W9-BYJ-541

EVERYDAY LEARNING

E V E R Y D A Y
GRAMMAR
— MADE EASY —

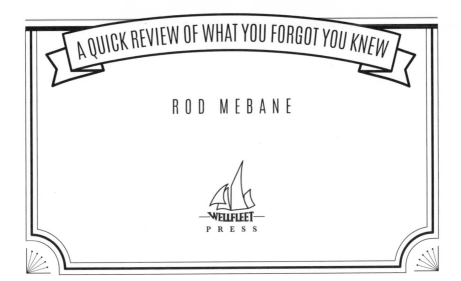

A QUICK REVIEW OF WHAT YOU FORGOT YOU KNEW

ROD MEBANE

WELLFLEET
PRESS

Inspiring | Educating | Creating | Entertaining

Brimming with creative inspiration, how-to projects, and useful information to enrich your everyday life, Quarto Knows is a favorite destination for those pursuing their interests and passions. Visit our site and dig deeper with our books into your area of interest: Quarto Creates, Quarto Cooks, Quarto Homes, Quarto Lives, Quarto Drives, Quarto Explores, Quarto Gifts, or Quarto Kids.

First published in 2021 by Wellfleet Press,
an imprint of The Quarto Group
142 West 36th Street, 4th Floor
New York, NY 10018, USA
T (212) 779-4972 F (212) 779-6058
www.QuartoKnows.com

DEDICATION:
To Donna, my travel partner, who has taught me the vocabulary of love along the way.

Wellfleet Press titles are also available at discount for retail, wholesale, promotional, and bulk purchase. For details, contact the Special Sales Manager by email at specialsales@quarto.com or by mail at The Quarto Group, Attn: Special Sales Manager, 100 Cummings Center Suite 265D, Beverly, MA 01915 USA.

10 9 8 7 6 5 4 3 2 1

ISBN: 978-1-57715-227-9

Library of Congress Control Number: 2021933256

Publisher: Rage Kindelsperger
Creative Director: Laura Drew
Managing Editor: Cara Donaldson
Senior Editor: John Foster
Cover and Interior Design: Amelia LeBarron

Printed in China

INTRODUCTION

I once asked a handyman friend of mine what his favorite tool was, and he answered without hesitation, "the oscillating saw." I was a little surprised that he answered so quickly, and that he could be so sure, but I was a lot surprised that he named a tool I had never heard of. Since I fancy myself as a pretty passable handyman knockoff, I promptly looked into the tool, bought a decent model, and now my best buddy, the O-saw, is the darling of my workshop too. I can do things with the O-saw that I never thought possible. And that's the point—one that's been driven home again and again over my tool-using years: You cannot even know what is possible until you know what the tools available to you can do. And that's how I think about grammar and language.

Words are construction tools—we manipulate them like building blocks to express thoughts for sharing with others—and you can do amazing things with words, but, as my tool story illustrates, only if you know what they can do.

There are two key tools for how our language works. The first is **vocabulary**—the words themselves (also referred to as the **lexicon**). The second is **grammar**—the principles that guide how words work together. These two tools are available to you, essentially free of charge. In the vocabulary arena, there are over 200,000 or so words in the English language. Any good dictionary will get you well down that road. In the grammar area, there are tons of reliable sources, many just a click or two away, that will give way more information than you could ever want to know.

Yet, even with an abundant supply of language resources, most people are not super-confident in their English-language skills, and that is where *Everyday Grammar* aims to find a happy home. If you count yourself among those who could benefit with a bit of everyday grammar improvement, the main focus of this book is on you and your capabilities. It is structured to reinforce your foundational understanding of grammar, spark your curiosity, and solidify your confidence.

People come to English grammar in a number of different ways. Natural-born English speakers first learn language rules by mimicking older family members. Individuals learning English as a second or third language rely on the structure of their native language as a frame of reference. In schools, students receive vastly different grammar experiences, ranging from cursory treatment of the underlying grammar fundamentals to the precise old-school rigors of diagramming sentences.

In light of these different starting points, the *Everyday Grammar* approach is to create a new beginning for everyone. We take it from the top to present a common big-picture overview and then move to establish a foundation for organizing and understanding the minute details that make up the world of grammar.

At the outset, it should be noted that this book is *not* meant to be a "one-stop shop." There is way too much information related to grammar to fit in this handy little volume. Instead, the practical goal is to create a framework for mastering basic grammar principles. In Part I, **Fundamentals**, you will find a quick presentation of basic grammar concepts. Then, in Part II, **In-Depth Focus**, there is a deeper dive into the various parts of speech and the underlying principles that guide how the different grammar parts work together. Finally, in Part III, **Common Pitfalls**, many of the most common grammar and spelling errors that people make are detailed, complete with right and wrong examples. To supplement the core, the following appendices are also included at the back of the book:

- Appendix A contains an extensive **Glossary of Grammar Terms** that is vital to grasping the many key concepts of grammar and the interrelationships of all the parts.

- Appendix B presents **Verb Guides** containing highly useful data in a quick look-up format such as complete profiles (aka conjugations) of key verbs and an extensive lists of regular and irregular verbs.

- Appendix C points the way to **Useful Grammar Resources** with numerous additional sources of information and knowledge on English grammar.

If you are new to learning aspects of grammar in a serious way, *Everyday Grammar* is presented in a natural flow that you can follow to build your knowledge in a systematic way. If you are experienced with grammar but just need a refresher, this book works as an excellent reference resource.

The many specifics associated with grammar are not a secret. Just search Google and you will venture into a language land of plenty in which there is no shortage of answers to be found. But, for the inexperienced grammar traveler, a big first challenge is to know what to look for and what questions to ask. This book is written to provide the foundation for asking good grammar-related questions. As you prepare to learn or review the basics of grammar, here are some important perspectives to keep in mind:

- Language is alive and constantly evolving—both in vocabulary (lexicon) and accepted usage (grammar).

- The evolutionary tendency in grammar has been to ease restrictions and to loosen the definition of what is acceptable.

- Lots of effective communication occurs without polished grammar.

- Your grammar does *not* have to be perfect. (*Psst:* No one's is.)

- You know more about grammar than you think.

- An important aspect of acquiring better grammar skills is unlearning past behaviors.

- If you improve your command of grammar, *you* are the primary beneficiary . . . *every day*!

As much as I hope you can leverage *Everyday Grammar* to pick up new skills, I hope even more that you can bulk up confidence in your language-creation abilities and develop a passion for learning more.

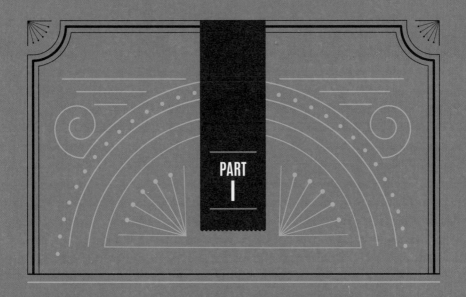

PART
I

FUNDAMENTALS

CHAPTER I

GRAMMAR BASICS

Grammar is nothing more than a set of rules that specifies how we use words to communicate. This seems harmless enough, but for many people the word *grammar* comes with a bad reputation. It is probably best left to psychologists to give good reasons for its bad rep, but suffice it to say that the mere mention of grammar can prompt winces and groans and quickly thin a crowd. Yet, here you are, not only holding but also reading this book, suggesting there is something about the topic that interests you enough to get this far . . . Welcome! The main point of *Everyday Grammar* is to make it easier for you to become more familiar with grammar in general and better at using grammar in *everyday* situations. If you share this goal, then together we can demystify some of the confusing aspects of grammar and make it start working better for you.

— GRAMMAR AND YOU —

An important observation at the outset is that regardless of how much you care about grammar, it is totally indifferent to you. Grammar does not "give a hoot" about how well you understand the underlying language rules or how well you use them. Grammar is just the set of rules. It is up to you (and every individual) to determine your relationship with the rules and the extent to which you will pay attention to them. If you are looking for good reasons to strengthen your grammar skills, look no further. As you reflect on this commitment to grammar principles, here are a few things to take into consideration:

- Grammar is essential to you (and to all of us).

- Grammar is a critical contributor to your personal brand.

- Grammar directly influences your clarity of thought and power of expression.

─ NECESSITY OF GRAMMAR ─

For someone who is not a big fan of grammar, there may be a desire just to wish it away, but that simply is not possible for any of us—as long as we want to communicate with one another. Our ability to communicate is a hallmark of being human, and our communication relies on a meaningful exchange of thoughts. In order to make that exchange and get a thought out of our brain and meaningfully into someone else's, we need to use some kind of intervening code—an identified set of sounds and/or symbols that are commonly recognized and understood by the parties involved.

In our communication, we rely on many different codes (Morse code, American Sign Language, emoticons, body language) to exchange meaning among ourselves, but by far the most dominant code in our everyday lives is our local everyday language.

In this context, grammar is the accepted set of everyday language rules that enable the common understanding among us that is needed to foster communication and the exchange of meaning. Without grammar, there is no common understanding. Without understanding, there is no communication. Quite plainly, we need to communicate, and we need the rules of grammar. Of course, how rigorously the rules are enforced varies depending on the situation. For example, there are some frequent everyday contexts in which people are not expected to follow grammar rules too strictly, such as:

- In regular conversation with friends and family members, people speak informally and without the same rigor or structure that you might see in writing or in more formal social settings.

- In the world of social networking—texting, tweeting, and the like—it is practically the Wild West of "anything goes" for grammar, spelling, and language conventions in general.

- When traveling abroad, it is remarkable to see how much good communication can happen with a combination of sounds, hand gestures, and picture drawing . . . and not much grammar.

However, in many everyday contexts—such as correspondence, public remarks, business interactions (meetings, memos, emails, presentations), funding proposals, marketing materials, and numerous social situations—grammar rules do apply more formally, and those conditions tend to favor those who demonstrate a good command of grammar, both in speaking and in writing.

In other aspects of life—such as various professions and trades, the arts, the sports world, and so forth—we often have choices as to what fields of endeavor we will commit to and how well we will learn the vocabulary and rules associated with those fields. That is *not* the case with language, which is a field in which we have no choice. If we want to communicate with others, we have to know some grammar basics. In short, regardless of the formality or informality of the communication setting, some working knowledge of grammar is essential.

– VISIBILITY OF GRAMMAR –

Rules of accepted behavior abound in virtually every field of human endeavor. A scientist who adheres to the discipline of the scientific method, a baseball manager who knows to argue a ground-rule double, a concert violinist who leads from her chair, a STEM or STEAM teacher who discovers a new experiential way for children to learn—these are people who are experts in their fields partly because they know, understand, and follow the relevant "rules of the game."

Unlike in other fields of endeavor—as in science or sports or music or education—when it comes to language, you cannot hide or keep your expertise (or lack thereof) to yourself. Your grammar skills accompany you wherever you go, and they are revealed in every conversation you have, every talk you give, every observation you post, and every item you write.

Not surprisingly, given its visibility and prominence, your communication behavior will affect how others perceive you. Like other attributes—your tone of voice, gestures, and manner of dress—how you communicate will be an important influence on the impression that you create on others. If you regularly expose grammatical errors in your speaking and writing, those errors will be noticed. They will make an impression, and the judgments that others make about you may not be favorable. For example, those who recognize basic grammar errors in your communication may conclude that you are not attentive to details (regardless of what the truth may be).

The flip side of this situation, of course, is also true. To the extent that you demonstrate capability in your command of vocabulary and grammar, it will be noticed. The perception of this proficiency is likely to boost your credibility by conveying the sense that "you know what you're talking about." How other people feel about you may or may not be important to you, but it is important at least to recognize that your language behavior affects the impressions people form about you.

— CLARITY OF THOUGHT —

As mentioned, language is our everyday tool for sharing thoughts with others, and grammar is the aspect of language that guides how the parts of language (especially words) work together. Effective communication depends on more than good word selection and correct application of grammar principles. In general, the more you command the underlying grammar resources and tools, the more you can be deliberate in your crafting of messages and in your communication with others.

This knowledge principle is wonderfully illustrated by a young child learning language for the first time. It is easy to take language skills for granted as an older person, but observing a toddler learning the words *mama* or *book*, or later learning how *owls hoot* and *horses run*, brings the challenge (and delight) of language learning into full focus.

Of special relevance in this context is the interrelationship between a child's ability to think clearly of a *horse* and the child's ability to know and say the word *horse*. From a developmental standpoint, those two abilities go hand in hand. And, as the child grows and learns, language sophistication grows along with the child's ability to conceptualize and understand—as the child learns about different kinds of horses, for example, or about aspects of how they live.

In short, your underlying knowledge of language—vocabulary and grammar—is an important determiner of what you think about, how you think, and how you choose to communicate with others. Consequently, there is a definite upside to enhancing grammar knowledge and skill, with such benefits as:

- It reduces errors that other people notice and find annoying and distracting.

- It creates an impression that you are organized in your thinking and committed to quality.

- It conveys a sense of someone who is well educated and prepared, which bolsters your credibility.

- It allows for communication enriched in thought, precision, and quality of expression—in both your speaking and your writing.

- It creates a more polished and persuasive appearance in your written pieces, from job-seeking letters to business proposals to advocacy statements.

- Lastly, in terms of your interactions with others, stronger grammar knowledge and skills often lead to generally higher levels of self-confidence and interpersonal effectiveness.

CHAPTER 2

THE BUILDING BLOCKS OF LANGUAGE

As noted in the introduction, words can be thought of as construction tools that we manipulate like building blocks to express thoughts to share with others. The words themselves make up our **vocabulary**, or **lexicon**. The principles that govern the structuring of words in order to create meaning make up our **grammar**. Vocabulary and grammar are the two key ingredients necessary for good communication. One without the other is of little use. Consider the following vocabulary words, in alphabetical order:

and	*love*	*sings*	*woman*
beautifully	*quietly*	*the*	*young*
in	*she*	*touching*	

Each of these words has definitions unto itself, but the group of words as a whole does not convey any specific meaning. However, if the words are sorted in a manner consistent with principles of grammar, they might shake out as follows:

The young woman in love—she sings quietly and beautifully. Touching!

Now this group of words is meaningful!

— CREATING A COMPLETE THOUGHT —

In terms of the building blocks of language, words are numerous. Within the category of words, there are eight parts of speech, each of which has governing principles that we will look at a bit later in this chapter. These parts of speech, and the many words within each, come together in countless ways to create

THE GRAMMAR HIERARCHY

The grammar hierarchy of significance is expressed as follows: (1) combinations of **letters** form **words**; (2) combinations of words form **phrases** and **clauses**; and (3) all of the basic language elements—letters, words, phrases, and clauses—are the building blocks that come together in a **sentence** to create meaning. In communicating with others, it is meaning that we seek to convey, and it is meaning that we seek in return. In order to create a meaningful exchange, we need to understand these basic building blocks.

BUILDING BLOCK	EXAMPLE
Letters: the Roman Latin alphabet of twenty-six letters (in both upper- and lowercase)	*XYZ, abc*
Word: a combination of letters that form one of the eight parts of speech	*dog*
Phrase: a group of related words *without* a clear subject and associated verb	*the barking dog*
Clause: a group of related words with a clear subject and associated verb	*the dog barks*
Sentence: a clause that is sensible as a stand-alone group of words, with appropriate punctuation	*The dog barks.*

larger units of meaning that themselves are mixed to create a final sentence. (See The Building Blocks of Grammar on page 16 to get a sense of all of the underlying parts.) Within this abundance of information, it is useful to focus on the most fundamental principle of grammar: In order to create meaning, you must organize your words to present a **complete thought**. The test for whether a group of words presents a complete thought is straightforward. At a minimum, a complete thought: (1) requires a subject and a predicate, and (2) must be sensible standing on its own. Let's look at these components more closely.

The **subject** is the entity that is *doing something* or *being something* in the thought. The subject always is or contains a noun (more on nouns in chapter 3).

The **predicate** is the experience that is *happening* to the subject. The predicate always is or contains a verb (more on verbs in chapter 6).

SUBJECT	+	PREDICATE	=	COMPLETE THOUGHT
raindrops	+	*fall*	=	*Raindrops fall.*
the athlete	+	*runs fast*	=	*The athlete runs fast.*

Note that, in terms of order and sequence, the subject generally (but not always) comes before the predicate (which is or contains a verb). The following sections of this chapter amplify aspects of these important building blocks to strengthen your familiarity with key concepts and to build your skills in applying everyday grammar principles in speaking and writing.

QUICK TEST: HOW TO DETERMINE THE SUBJECT AND PREDICATE

To determine the **subject** of a sentence, ask and answer the question: *What is this sentence about?* To determine the **predicate** of a sentence, ask and answer these questions: *What is the subject? What is/was the subject doing? What is/was happening to the subject?*

The cow jumped over the moon.

Subject Question: *What is the sentence about?*	Answer: *the cow*
Predicate Question: *What was happening to the subject?*	Answer: *It jumped over the moon.*

— THE BUILDING BLOCKS OF GRAMMAR —

Below is a quick guide of the fundamental building blocks of grammar that we will cover in the remaining part of this chapter:

Parts of Speech: noun; adjective; pronoun; verb; adverb; conjunction; preposition; interjection

Phrases: noun phrase; verb phrase; infinitive phrase; gerund phrase; participle phrase; prepositional phrase; absolute phrase; appositive phrase

Clauses: independent clause; dependent clause; adverb clause; adjective clause; noun clause

Objects: direct object; indirect object

Sentences: simple; compound; complex; compound-complex; statement; question; command; exclamation

— PARTS OF SPEECH —

Like shapes of puzzle pieces or colors of blocks, there are different types of words. In English grammar, there are eight types of words available to mix in different ways to create meaning. We refer to the eight types as **parts of speech** and introduce them to you briefly here. You will have the opportunity to learn more about them and how they interact in later chapters. Since grammar principles of association are organized around the parts of speech, understanding the parts of speech is at the heart of understanding grammar. Let's recast our first example on page 13 in different colors so that we can color-code the eight parts of speech in English:

The young woman in love—she sings quietly and beautifully. Touching!

(1) NOUNS: Nouns are always the stars of the show, because nouns are the words we use to **name things**—like *horse, ball, ocean, house.* In the

English language, hundreds of thousands of nouns are available to name people and places, animals and activities, ideas, and emotions—all sorts of things. (See more on nouns in chapter 3.)

(2) ADJECTIVES: Adjectives can be thought of as modifiers for nouns because they always accompany nouns and provide additional **description**—like color (*blue sky*) or age (*young calf*) or mood (*sad boy*). A simple change in adjective can make a world of difference in meaning, as in *thriving planet* versus *dying planet*. (See more on adjectives in chapter 4.)

(3) PRONOUNS: After being introduced, a noun can take a break while a pronoun is used instead to **refer to the noun** involved. A pronoun is a word that can step in to take the place of a noun when appropriate, such as *The woman joined the choir. She sings alto.* (See more on pronouns in chapter 5.)

(4) VERBS: Verbs are where the **action** is. Literally, nothing happens without verbs, whether the happening is an action, an event, a condition, or simply a state of being. Through variations in **tense** (*i.e.*, if the action happens in the past, present, or future), verbs also indicate the general **time frame** in which a happening occurs, such as *John is walking now* (PRESENT); *John walked yesterday* (PAST); *and John will walk tomorrow* (FUTURE). There are over 25,000 different verbs available in English. (See more on verbs in chapter 6.)

(5) ADVERBS: Verbs frequently have companions called adverbs. These words can often be quite dramatic in labeling a variety of **circumstances associated** with a verb's action, such as *Her heart beat wildly*. Adverbs often answer the questions of *How? When? Where? How much? How often? How long?* (See more on adverbs in chapter 7.)

(6) CONJUNCTIONS: To make connections we use conjunctions, which exist exactly for that purpose—to **connect** words, phrases, clauses, and/ or sentences. There are only a handful of words that serve as the primary coordinating conjunctions—*and*, *but*, *or*, *nor*, *for*, *so*, and *yet*—but there are other conjunctions that serve in specific situations. (See more on conjunctions in chapter 8.)

(7) PREPOSITIONS: A preposition is a word that comes before a noun or pronoun to **form a prepositional phrase** that is itself used to modify a noun, adverb, or adjective. *Which woman? The woman in love.* There are more than 150 words that serve as prepositions, although a fifth of those (around 30) are used most frequently, including *through*, *to*, *on*, *over*, *around*, *under*, *by*, *behind*, *below*, *in*, and *along*, to name a few. (See more on prepositions in chapter 8.)

(8) INTERJECTIONS: To express **strong emotion**, such as joy, surprise, anger, or enthusiasm, an interjection is a word (or phrase) that is usually used in isolation in an exclamatory way, such as *Whoops! Aha! Yikes!* (See more on interjections in chapter 8.)

WHAT IS A MODIFIER?

A modifier is a word, phrase, or clause that serves to add information to another word in order to clarify, explain, emphasize, limit, or enhance the meaning. Some modifiers serve as **adjectives** in modifying nouns:

> Sarah, *a new mom*, longs for a *full night's* sleep.

Other modifiers serve as **adverbs** in modifying verbs, adjectives, and other adverbs:

> John enjoyed working out *intensely at the beach*.
> Her recovery story was *remarkably* moving.
> The doctor inserted the tube *very* carefully.

— PHRASES —

A **phrase** is a combination of words that works as a single grammatical unit but does *not* contain a subject and a predicate with an associated verb. There are eight types of phrases, and among the most common are noun phrases and verb phrases:

(1) A **noun phrase** is a combination of words that includes a **noun** and all of **its modifiers**. In the example *The athlete runs fast*, *the athlete* is a noun phrase, and the entire phrase serves as the subject of the complete thought.

QUICK TEST: HOW TO DETERMINE A NOUN PHRASE

To test whether a combination of words is a noun phrase, replace the phrase with a pronoun and determine if the sentence still makes sense. The following sentence contains two noun phrases—one serving as a subject, the other serving as a direct object:

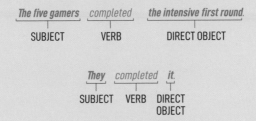

(2) A **verb phrase** is a combination of words that includes a **verb** and all of **its modifiers**. In the example *The athlete runs fast*, *runs fast* is a verb phrase, and the entire phrase serves as the predicate of the complete thought.

(3) An **infinitive phrase** is a combination of words that starts with the **infinitive** of a verb and serves as a noun.

> *To walk the talk* *can be difficult to do.*

(4) A **gerund phrase** is a combination of words that starts with the **gerund** of a verb and serves as a noun.

> *Singing in the rain* *is more fun than it sounds.*

(5) **A participle phrase** is a combination of words that starts with the **present participle** or **past participle** of a verb and always serves as an adjective.

> *The carpenter* ***working on the cabinets*** *decided to take a short break.*

(6) A **prepositional phrase** is a combination of words that include a **preposition**, an **object of the preposition**, and any modifiers. If a prepositional phrase modifies a noun, it is called an **adjective prepositional phrase**.

> *The house* ***at the end*** *was the first to be built.*

If a prepositional phrase modifies a verb, it is called an **adverb prepositional phrase**.

> *The little girl tried not to sneeze* ***in her kindergarten class***.

(7) An **absolute phrase** is a combination of words that modifies an independent clause in its entirety.

> ***God willing***, *the family will survive their difficult circumstances.*

(8) An **appositive phrase** is a combination of words that renames or restates an adjacent word or phrase to provide additional information.

> *Willie,* ***the lazy dog***, *does not like the game of fetch.*

WHAT IS A COMPLEMENT?

In grammar, **complement** is a general term used to refer to a word, phrase, or clause that completes the meaning of an expression. A **subject complement** (aka **predicate nominative**) is a noun or pronoun that follows linking verbs (TO APPEAR, TO BE, TO FEEL, TO LOOK, etc.) and provides additional information about the subject.

*The doctor is an epidemiology **expert**.*

An **object complement** provides additional information about a direct object.

*The doctor inserted the syringe **filled with saline solution**.*

– CLAUSES –

Unlike a phrase, a **clause** includes a subject and a predicate with an associated verb, and there are two main types of clauses:

(1) An **independent** (or **main**) **clause** is a clause containing a subject and a verb that conveys a complete thought and **can stand** by itself. No additional information is needed to create a complete thought.

Nik and Valerie waited in line.

(2) A **dependent** (or **subordinate**) **clause** is a clause containing a subject and a verb that does *not* convey a complete thought and thus ***cannot* stand** by itself.

While Nik and Valerie waited in line...

With a dependent clause, additional information is required to create a complete thought.

While Nik and Valerie waited in line, the venue sold out of tickets.

INDEPENDENT CLAUSES
VERSUS SENTENCES

By definition, an **independent clause** by itself is a sentence. It meets the minimum requirements of what it takes to be a sentence—it has a subject and a predicate and is sensible standing alone.

The Declaration of Independence is one of the most important documents in history.

        SUBJECT   PREDICATE

On the other hand, a **sentence** can contain much more than a single independent clause. Sentences can be simple (as in the example above) or designated as compound, complex, and compound-complex (see pages 25-26).

We hold these truths to be self-evident, that all men are created equal,

    INDEPENDENT CLAUSE   DEPENDENT CLAUSE 1

that they are endowed by their Creator with certain unalienable Rights,

DEPENDENT CLAUSE 2

that among these are Life, Liberty and the pursuit of Happiness.

DEPENDENT CLAUSE 3

Within the category of **dependent clauses**, there are three different subtypes:

(1) An a**dverb clause** is a dependent clause that functions as an adverb.

> *After the concert ended, Jason trekked to his vintage VW camper.*

(2) An **adjective clause** is a dependent clause that functions as an adjective.

> *Aiko, **who is a "dry mouth" St. Bernard**, drooled when Jason returned.*

(3) A **noun clause** is a dependent clause that functions as a noun.

Whoever planned the concert tour did a first-class job.

− OBJECTS −

The predicate of the sentence, which includes the verb, may also include **objects**—nouns or pronouns that receive the action of the verb either directly (**direct objects**) or indirectly (**indirect objects**). Consider the following sentence:

Benjamin   *gave*   *Alexandra*   *a*   *ring.*
SUBJECT   VERB   INDIRECT OBJECT   DIRECT OBJECT

The **subject** of the sentence is *Benjamin.*

The **verb** of the sentence is *gave.*

The **direct object** of the verb is *ring.*
(Ring directly receives the action of the verb GAVE—a ring is what Benjamin gave.)

The **indirect object** of the verb is *Alexandra.*
(Alexandra is affected by the action of the verb, but is not the primary, direct object, which is the ring.)

Note that as an indirect object *Alexandra* can be removed from the sentence, and the sentence still expresses a complete thought (though a different one), as in *Benjamin gave a ring*. This is not the case if the direct object is removed from the sentence, as in *Benjamin gave Alexandra*, which is not a complete, sensible thought. In summary, the subject of the sentence is *Benjamin*, and the predicate of the sentence is *gave Alexandra a ring*, which includes a direct object (*ring*) and an indirect object (*Alexandra*).

— SENTENCES —

A complete thought is expressed in a unit called a **sentence**. Minimally, a sentence requires a subject and a predicate, and it must make sense standing on its own. As we saw earlier, an **independent clause** meets these requirements, and an independent clause just by itself is called a simple sentence.

Dogs bark.

INDEPENDENT CLAUSE

In terms of internal structure, an independent clause (aka simple sentence) generally falls into one of seven different patterns:

1	**SUBJECT**	**VERB**		
	Lisa	raked		
2	**SUBJECT**	**VERB**	**SUBJECT COMPLEMENT**	
	Lisa	is	a gardener	
3	**SUBJECT**	**VERB**	**DIRECT OBJECT**	
	Lisa	raked	the garden	
4	**SUBJECT**	**VERB**	**DIRECT OBJECT**	**OBJECT COMPLEMENT**
	Lisa	raked	the garden	covered by weeds
5	**SUBJECT**	**VERB**	**ADVERBIAL †**	
	Lisa	raked	feverishly	
6	**SUBJECT**	**VERB**	**DIRECT OBJECT**	**ADVERBIAL †**
	Lisa	raked	the garden	feverishly
7	**SUBJECT**	**VERB**	**INDIRECT OBJECT**	**DIRECT OBJECT**
	Lisa	gave	Daniel	the rake

---

† ***Adverbial*** *is a general term used to refer to an adverb, adverb phrase, or adverb clause that completes the meaning of an expression. An adverbial provides additional information about the verb.*

Structurally, there are four kinds of sentences:

(1) A **simple sentence** consists of just one independent clause, which makes sense as a complete thought on its own.

The dog barked.

INDEPENDENT CLAUSE

(2) A **compound sentence** consists of two or more independent clauses, usually joined by a coordinating conjunction.

The dog barked,   and   baby Jackson cried.

INDEPENDENT   COORDINATING   INDEPENDENT
CLAUSE 1   CONJUNCTION   CLAUSE 2

(3) A **complex sentence** consists of at least one independent clause and at least one dependent clause that does not make sense on its own (dependent clauses many times begin with subordinating conjunctions, shown with *while* in the example below).

*Baby Jackson cried   **while** the dog barked.*

INDEPENDENT CLAUSE   DEPENDENT CLAUSE

PUNCTUATION TIP

In writing, a sentence is typically denoted by an initial capital letter and a concluding punctuation mark—a period (.), question mark (?), or exclamation point (!):

Raindrops fall.   Does the athlete run fast?   Give Calvin his toy now!

SUBORDINATING CONJUNCTIONS

In a complex sentence, a subordinating conjunction always introduces the dependent clause and identifies the type of relationship. (See more on conjunctions in chapter 8.) Some common subordinating conjunctions include:

although	if	than	until
as	since	that	while
because	so that	unless	

(4) A **compound-complex sentence** is a compound sentence consisting of two or more independent clauses, at least one of which includes a dependent clause

While the dog barked, *baby Jackson cried,* *and* *the sitter wondered what to do.*

| DEPENDENT CLAUSE | INDEPENDENT CLAUSE 1 | COORDINATING CONJUNCTION | INDEPENDENT CLAUSE 2 |

Substantively, a sentence can have one of four purposes and thus can be one of four types, as detailed in this table:

PURPOSE	SENTENCE TYPE	FORMAT NOTES	EXAMPLE
(1) Makes a STATEMENT	Declarative	Always ends with a period (.)	*That is Calvin's toy.*
(2) Asks a QUESTION	Interrogative	Always ends with a question mark (?)	*Is that Calvin's toy?*
(3) Issues a COMMAND	Imperative	Can end with a period (.) or an exclamation mark (!)	*Give Calvin his toy!*
(4) Expresses an EXCLAMATION	Exclamatory	Typically ends with an exclamation mark (!)	*Now!*

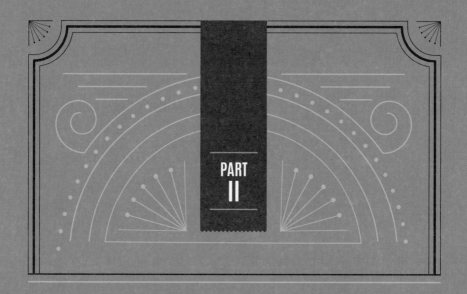

PART
II

IN-DEPTH
FOCUS

CHAPTER 3

FOCUS ON NOUNS

Nouns are *always* the stars of the show, because nouns are the words we use to name things. Hundreds of thousands of nouns are available to name people and places, animals and activities, ideas, and emotions—all sorts of things. Nouns are extremely versatile. There are a number of different types of nouns. Attesting to their versatility, nouns often serve in a subject role, but they also serve as objects (direct and indirect) and can even work as adjectives.

At the highest level, there are two major categories of nouns: (1) a **proper noun** names a particular person, place, or thing (*Santa Claus*, *Vietnam*, *Chicago Bulls*) while (2) a **common noun** does not name a particular person, place, or thing (*holiday*, *country*, *team*). Note that a proper noun is *always* capitalized regardless of where it falls in a sentence. A common noun is typically only capitalized when it appears at the start of a sentence. Within the much larger category of common nouns, there are some subtypes that grammarians regularly identify, including:

(1) **Collective nouns** identify a group (*a **swarm** of bees*, *an **army** of ants*).

(2) **Compound nouns** are nouns made up of a combination of at least two words: *sailboat* (sail + boat), *earthquake* (earth + quake), *honeydew* (honey + dew).

PUNCTUATION TIP

Some word combinations that function as nouns call for a hyphen, as in *roller-skating*, *sister-in-law*. Others show a space between the words, as in *swimming pool, attorney general*. The rules for when to combine the words and when to use spaces or hyphens are inconsistent. When in doubt, look it up in a dictionary or online!

(3) A **concrete noun** is a noun that can be experienced by one of our five senses of sight, sound, touch, smell, or taste (*pizza*). An **abstract noun**, on the other hand, names something that is an idea, a quality, or a state that you cannot sense directly (*truth*).

(4) A **countable noun** refers to items that can be counted (*eggs*), while an **uncountable noun** refers to a more general concept that cannot be counted (*happiness*). Uncountable nouns generally *cannot* be made plural (*knowledges* is incorrect).

MAKING NOUNS PLURAL

To make a noun plural, add an **-s** at the end of the word (book + s = books) *unless* the single noun ends in: **-s**, **-ss**, **-sh**, **-ch**, **-es**, **-x**, or **-z**. In such a case, you should add **-es** to the end of the word (church + es = churches).

– VERBAL FORMS –
THAT FUNCTION AS NOUNS

The infinitive phrase and the gerund phrase are two **verbal forms** that serve as nouns. An infinitive is the base form of the verb with the preposition *to*, as in TO PAINT. An **infinitive phrase** can be used as a noun to refer to the act of painting as seen in this example.

To paint is to renew.
(USED AS A NOUN)

A **gerund phrase** is the present participle form of a verb (the -*ing* form) that is used as a noun. Consider the verb TO RUN. The present participle used to express the act in progress is *running*. If you take the same word and treat the act of running as a type of action (as opposed to an action in progress), then it becomes a noun that can be used as a subject, object, or subject complement (aka predicate nominative).

Running is an efficient form of exercise.
(USED AS THE SUBJECT)
An efficient form of exercise is running.
(USED AS THE SUBJECT COMPLEMENT)

MAKING NOUNS POSSESSIVE

To make a noun possessive, add an apostrophe + s (**'s**) at the end of a singular noun.

library → library's
cactus → cactus's

If the noun is plural and ends in s, add just an apostrophe (**'**) at the end.

animals → animals'

Add an apostrophe + s (**'s**) if the plural noun ends in any other letter.

children → children's

CHAPTER 4

FOCUS ON ADJECTIVES

Adjectives can be thought of as modifiers because they always accompany nouns and typically provide additional description—like color (*green pastures*) or age (*teen leader*) or mood (*angry birds*). A simple change of adjective can make a world of difference in meaning, as in an *adoring* crowd versus an *aggressive* crowd. Adjectives modify nouns and give us information about nouns. They answer such questions like: *How many? What kind? What color? Which one?* The options are voluminous, with over five thousand different adjectives available to give additional information on nouns.

QUICK TEST: HOW TO IDENTIFY AN ADJECTIVE IN A SENTENCE

Use this quick test to easily identify an adjective in any sentence.

STEP 1. Determine the word or phrase that is described/modified/informed (the target).

> The **black** <u>stallion</u> in Lane 3 raced quickly down the stretch.

STEP 2. Ask: *Is the target a noun?*

IF NO	=	MODIFIER IS NOT AN ADJECTIVE.
IF YES	=	MODIFIER IS PROBABLY AN ADJECTIVE, proceed.

STEP 3. Ask: *Does the word in question answer any of the questions: What kind? How many? Which one?*

IF NO	=	MODIFIER IS NOT AN ADJECTIVE.
IF YES	=	MODIFIER IS AN ADJECTIVE.

> What kind of stallion? A **black** stallion.

Most adjectives are thought of as **descriptive adjectives**. As suggested in the name, these adjectives describe the noun and expand its meaning—they elaborate on characteristics of the noun. For example, let's consider the noun *apple*. How might we describe and expand the meaning of an apple? Color is important (*The apple is **red***). And shape (*The red apple is **round***). And size (*The red, round apple is **big***). And condition (*The big, red, round apple is **fresh***). All of these are examples of descriptive adjectives.

There is also a significant group of adjectives called **limiting adjectives**. These are words that tell us something that helps define the specificity or identity of a noun, as opposed to describing characteristics of the noun (*Is it **a** church or **the** church? Is it **this** cupcake or **that** cupcake?*) Within the category of limiting adjectives, there are nine different types:

(1) Definite and Indefinite Articles

the, a, an

An article is a word used before a noun to indicate its state of definiteness (or specificity). The article *the* is a **definite article** (*the* store). The articles *a* and *an* are **indefinite articles** (*a* book, *an* apple).

(2) Demonstrative Adjectives

this, that, these, those

A demonstrative adjective is a word used before a noun to indicate a state of greater specificity than what an article would provide.

*Do you want **this** cookie? No, I want **that** one.*
*Have you visited **these** countries? Yes, I have visited **those** countries and lots more.*

(3) Interrogative Adjectives

who, whose, what, which, whom

An interrogative adjective is a word that modifies a noun at the beginning of a question (aka interrogative sentence).

__What__ game should Andrew play first? __Which__ candidate should Vicki support?
__Whose__ paintings are the most expressive?

(4) Relative Adjectives

what, which, whose, whatever, whichever, whosever

A relative adjective is a word that modifies a noun when introducing a clause that involves a choice or alternative.

*Tim couldn't decide **which** path to take.*
*The Book Club will read **whatever** book the host selects.*

(5) Numerical Adjectives   cardinals (one, two, three, etc.)
                                            ordinals (first, second, third, etc.)

A numerical adjective is either a cardinal number used with a noun to indicate a specific quantity or amount, or an ordinal number used with a noun to indicate position, degree, or rank in a sequence.

*Alexis has lived in at least **three** states.*
*Stella was the **second** St. Bernard to join the family.*

(6) Quantifiers   all, any, enough, few, less, least, a little, a lot of, many, more, most,
                           much, no, none, not any, plenty of, several, some (and many more)

A quantifier is a word or phrase used before a noun to indicate quantity or amount *in general*. The most common are above.

*There were just **enough** cookies to go around.*

(7) Possessive Adjectives   my, your, their (noun's, nouns')

A possessive adjective is an adjective form of a noun used to show possession—a "belonging" relationship with another noun. It is created by adding an apostrophe + s at the end of the word or, if the noun ends in s, by just adding an apostrophe.

Alice's restaurant, worker's uniform
pilots' union, states' rights

(8) Comparative Adjectives   adjective-er (than), adjective-ier (than),
                                           more adjective (than)

A comparative adjective is used in the comparison of two nouns to indicate a quantity or quality difference between them. The conjunction *than* is often used in the comparison.

*Tom was older **than** Barbara by about a year.*
*Susan is **more aware** of raccoon movements **than** most.*

(9) Superlative Adjectives   adjective-est, adjective-iest, most adjective (of)

A superlative adjective is used in a comparison of nouns to identify a maximum or extreme level.

FORMING COMPARATIVE
AND SUPERLATIVE ADJECTIVES

The following tables provide guidelines for forming comparative and superlative adjectives.

REGULAR ADJECTIVES					
ADJECTIVE		**COMPARATIVE**		**SUPERLATIVE**	
One syllable	*Jackson is young.*	**add -er**	*Davis is younger.*	**add -est**	*Felix is the youngest.*
Two syllables ending in -y	*The pansy is pretty.*	**drop -y, add -ier**	*The daffodil is prettier.*	**drop -y, add -iest**	*The rose is the prettiest.*
Three or more syllables	*The biscuit was delicious.*	**more + adjective**	*The cookie was more delicious.*	**most + adjective**	*The eclair was most delicious.*

COMMON IRREGULAR ADJECTIVES					
ADJECTIVE		**COMPARATIVE**		**SUPERLATIVE**	
good	*Peas are good.*	**better**	*Tomatoes are better.*	**best**	*Brussels sprouts are best of all!*
well	*The well patient headed home.*	**better**	*The patient was better this morning.*	**best**	*The patient is presenting her best health.*
bad	*The flu was bad.*	**worse**	*Strep throat was worse.*	**worst**	*This year's flu strain is the worst.*
little	*A dollar is a little money.*	**less**	*A quarter is less money.*	**least**	*A penny is the least amount.*
far	*A far throw.*	**farther**	*Throw a farther toss.*	**the farthest**	*That was the farthest pass.*
far	*Far-reaching concept.*	**further**	*Without further adieu.*	**the furthest**	*She is the furthest ahead in the process.*

CHAPTER 5

FOCUS ON PRONOUNS AND CASE

Pronouns are words that step in to take the place of a noun when appropriate. After being introduced, a noun can take a break while a pronoun is used, instead, to refer to the noun. There are several different forms of pronouns. The most commonly used are personal pronouns—which stand in for people and things. In addition to personal pronouns, other pronoun forms that we will look at closely in this chapter include:

Personal Pronouns:	*Katy is now a college graduate.* **She** *majored in biology.*
Reflexive Pronouns:	*The injured* <u>man</u> *drove* **himself** *to the hospital.*
Reciprocal Pronouns:	*The* <u>children</u> *helped* **each other** *with distance learning.*
Indefinite Pronouns:	*There is* **nobody** *home.*
Relative Pronouns:	*The* <u>movie</u> **that** *you loved is streaming on Netflix.*
Demonstrative Pronouns:	**This** *is an award-winning dog.*
Interrogative Pronouns:	**What** *did the store owners decide to do?*

After we learn about the different types of pronouns, we will then look at case and its importance regarding which form of pronouns we use in different circumstances. Finally, we will then look at some guidelines on how to correctly use pronouns in their cases.

– PERSONAL PRONOUNS –

Personal pronouns stand in for people (aka **persons**) and sometimes things. There are three person types, and each has a singular and plural form (**number**). The person types are referred to with the ordinals first person, second person, and third person as follows:

First person refers to the speaker(s) in the sentence   I, we

Second person refers to the person(s) spoken to   you

Third person refers to the person(s) spoken about   he, she, it, they

ANTECEDENTS

The noun to which a pronoun refers is called the **antecedent**. The term stems from the Latin root word *ante* that means "going before."

Suzanne   left   *her*   briefcase at the office.
└──┬──┘   └┬┘
ANTECEDENT   PRONOUN

– CASE –

In addition to person and number, personal pronouns vary by a condition called case. **Case** is an important factor for how a pronoun serves in a sentence. There are three cases in English—subject case, object case, and possessive case—and each case has a set of pronoun forms. To follow common grammar principles, it is important to first recognize what case is and how it determines the appropriate pronoun form to use. For example, if a pronoun is in the **subject case**, then it is called a subject pronoun, and it takes a subject pronoun form. In the example *I bought John a coffee*, *I* is the subject of the sentence.

If a pronoun is in the **object case**, an object pronoun is required. In the example, *I bought **him** a coffee*, since the speaker is using *him* to refer to John, an object pronoun is required because it is functioning as the direct object.

Finally, if the pronoun is in the **possessive case**, a possessive pronoun is required to show ownership. In the example, *That coffee on the table is **his***, the speaker is indicating that the coffee on the table belongs to John. Let's look at the three cases a bit closer and their respective pronouns.

(1) **Subject Case:** When a pronoun is functioning as the **subject** or the **subject complement** (also called a **predicate nominative**), a **subject pronoun** is used for the appropriate person and number from the table below.

SUBJECT PRONOUNS		
PERSON	**NUMBER**	
	SINGULAR	*PLURAL*
First Person	I	we
Second Person	you	you
Third Person	he, she, it	they

__We__ will never get tired of bacon.
(WE = SUBJECT)
It was __he__ who started the fight.
(HE = PREDICATE NOMINATIVE)

PREDICATE NOMINATIVES
VERSUS PREDICATE ADJECTIVES

A **predicate nominative** is a noun or pronoun that follows a linking verb (see page 54) and functions as a subject complement.

*Robert is my **friend**.*

A **predicate adjective** is also a subject complement that is an adjective and follows a linking verb.

*Robert is **nice**.*

SUBJECT PRONOUNS AFTER LINKING VERBS

If a sentence calls for a pronoun to be used as a subject complement (aka predicate nominative) after a linking verb, the **subject case** of the pronoun should be used.

Nannie said, "Believe it or not, the cute little girl in that photo is I."

However, it is much more common to hear:

*Nannie said, "Believe it or not, the cute little girl in that photo is **me**."*

Some people feel the pure grammar construction in the first example sounds awkward and pretentious and prefer the second example. In spoken language, the second example is much more common.

(2) Object Case: When a pronoun is functioning as an object, either a **direct object**, **indirect object**, or **object of the preposition**, it takes an **object pronoun**, selected for the appropriate person and number from the table below.

OBJECT PRONOUNS		
PERSON	**NUMBER**	
	SINGULAR	*PLURAL*
First Person	me	us
Second Person	you	you
Third Person	him, her, it	them

*[You] give **us** a call when you get there.*
(US = DIRECT OBJECT)
*I gave **her** the letter.*
(HER = INDIRECT OBJECT)
*It won't happen if we depend on **them**.*
(THEM = OBJECT OF THE PREPOSITION)

(3) **Possessive Case:** When a pronoun indicates **possession** or **ownership**, it takes a **possessive pronoun**, selected for the appropriate person and number from the table below.

POSSESSIVE PRONOUNS		
PERSON	**NUMBER**	
	SINGULAR	*PLURAL*
First Person	mine	ours
Second Person	yours	yours
Third Person	his, hers, its*	theirs

* We only use the possessive pronoun *its* when *own* is also used (*That car has a life of **its own***).

*The <u>bike</u> was **mine** until I gave it away.*
(MINE = *I* OWN THE BIKE)

*In terms of <u>houses</u>, **theirs** was the most expensive.*
(THEIRS = *THEY* OWN THE HOUSES)

PUNCTUATION TIP

Note that **possessive pronouns** *never* take an apostrophe, as in *it's, our's,* or *your's*. These are incorrect.

— PRONOUNS IN ACTION —

Let's look at some examples of how pronouns vary in relation to person, number, and case depending on how they function in different sentences.

PERSON + NUMBER	CASE	EXAMPLE
First Person — Singular I, me, mine	Subject	*Finally, **I** am the champion!*
	Object	*My coach gave good advice to **me**.* [1]
	Possessive	*That sparkling new trophy is now **mine**.*
First Person — Plural we, us, ours	Subject	***We** will never get there in time.*
	Object	*Maybe the hosts will give **us** a break.* [3]
	Possessive	*If not, disappointment will be **ours**.*
Second Person — Singular you, you, yours	Subject	***You** are my sunshine.*
	Object	*I love **you** more than the moon is high.* [2]
	Possessive	*My tan is fading, but **yours** is still golden.*
Second Person — Plural you, you, yours	Subject	***You** are all welcome here.*
	Object	*The principal will talk to **you** next.* [1]
	Possessive	***Yours** is the best.*
Third Person — Singular he/she/it, him/her/it, his/hers/its	Subject	***She** left and never looked back.*
	Object	*The woman had given **him** the best years.* [3]
	Possessive	*In terms of confidence, **his** was shattered.*
Third Person — Plural they, them, theirs	Subject	***They** got tired of sheltering in place.*
	Object	*The nursing home bus took **them** for tests.* [2]
	Possessive	*Once the vaccine arrived, all of the residents got **theirs**.*

---

1 *Objects of the Preposition = Object Pronoun*

2 *Direct Objects = Object Pronoun*

3 *Indirect Objects = Object Pronoun*

POSSESSIVE PRONOUN ADJECTIVES

Similar to possessive pronouns are **possessive pronoun adjectives**, which are used when a pronoun is functioning as an **adjective** to express possession in a sentence. They are selected for appropriate person and number from the table below.

POSSESSIVE PRONOUN ADJECTIVES		
PERSON	**NUMBER**	
	SINGULAR	*PLURAL*
First Person	my	our
Second Person	your	your
Third Person	his, her, its	their

__My__ bike has gotten pretty small for me.
(MY = POSSESSIVE PRONOUN ADJECTIVE TO DESCRIBE *BIKE*)

__Their__ house will be put up for sale after it is painted.
(THEIR = POSSESSIVE PRONOUN ADJECTIVE TO DESCRIBE *HOUSE*)

OBJECT PRONOUNS USED WITH COMMON PREPOSITIONS

The preposition **between** and some others cause a lot of confusion. Because between is a preposition, pronouns that follow it are objects of the preposition and should therefore be in the object case.

Sally divided the money __between__ Bill and __me__.

QUICK TEST: PRONOUNS IN
COMPOUND CONSTRUCTIONS

Compound constructions are instances when there is either (1) more than one subject, such as *Bill and I went to the museum*, and the pronouns need to be in the subject case, or (2) when there is more than one object, direct object, indirect object, or object of the preposition, such as *John gave the museum tickets to Bill and me*, and the pronouns need to be in the object case.

Here is a simple test you can do to check to see which pronoun case is needed for a compound construction in the **subject case**. In our example, the compound construction is acting as the subject:

EXAMPLE: *Bill and (**I, me**) went to the museum.*

STEP 1.   Remove "Bill and"

STEP 2.   Ask yourself which pronoun reads better: "**Me** went to the museum" or "**I** went to the museum"?

STEP 3.   The correct answer is "**I** went to the museum," because *Bill* and *I* are both subjects and require the pronoun *I* to be in the subject case.

The same test can be applied for compound constructions in the **object case**. In our example, the compound construction is acting as a preposition phrase with two objects of the preposition:

EXAMPLE: *John gave the museum ticket to Bill and (**I, me**).*

STEP 1.   Remove "to Bill and"

STEP 2.   Ask yourself which pronoun reads better: "John gave the museum ticket to **I**" or "John gave the museum ticket to **me**"?

STEP 3.   The correct answer is "*John gave the museum ticket to Bill and **me**,*" because *Bill* and *me* are both objects of the preposition and require the pronoun *me* to be in the object case.

SECOND-PERSON PRONOUNS IN WRITING

When writing, the second-person pronouns—*you, your, yours, yourself, yourselves*—should only be used when directly addressing readers.

*Now we will introduce **you** to some new trends in fashion.*

It is not appropriate to use *you* when the reference is indefinite.

People have said that eating before swimming can make you sick.
(INCORRECT)

– REFLEXIVE PRONOUNS –

When the subject and the object of the verb are the same and refer to one another, a **reflexive pronoun** that "reflects" back to the subject is used in the object position, selected for appropriate person and number from the table below:

REFLEXIVE PRONOUNS		
PERSON	**NUMBER**	
	SINGULAR	*PLURAL*
First Person	myself	ourselves
Second Person	yourself	yourselves
Third Person	himself, herself, itself, oneself	themselves

*You will never forgive **yourselves** for failing to close the gate.*
(*YOURSELVES* RELATES BACK TO YOU)
*The oven is timed to turn off by **itself**.*
(*ITSELF* RELATES BACK TO OVEN)

— RECIPROCAL PRONOUNS —

A **reciprocal pronoun** is one that is used to indicate that a person(s) or thing(s) are involved in a mutual action or cross-relationship or when something is given or done in return. Reciprocal pronouns refer to individual items or a plural whole. There are only two reciprocal pronouns:

each other (used when there are two parties involved)
one another (used when there are more than two parties involved)

*Meg and Gary supported **each other** during the transition.*
*The winning team members gave **one another** elbow bumps in celebration.*

— INDEFINITE PRONOUNS —

An **indefinite pronoun** is a word that takes the place of a noun but does *not* refer to a specific person, time, or situation but to nonspecific people and items. Some of the words used most frequently in this "indefinite" way include:

SINGULAR	another, anybody, anyone, anything, each, either, everybody, everyone, everything, little, much, neither, no one, nobody, nothing, one, other, somebody, someone, something
PLURAL	both, few, many, others, several
SINGULAR/PLURAL	all, any, more, most, none, some

***Few** of the principals in town favor a full school reopening.*
*Medical professionals will test **everyone** in the community eventually.*

— RELATIVE PRONOUNS —

In sentences that have a **dependent** (or **subordinate**) **clause** (see pages 21-23), a **relative pronoun** may be used to introduce, or "relate," noun and adjective clauses to the rest of the sentence. The antecedent of the pronoun is usually identified. There are seven different words that commonly serve as relative pronouns:

that   which   who   whom   whose   whoever   whomever

*The book **that** <u>she loved</u> is no longer in print.*
*My son **whose** <u>dog is sick</u> headed to the vet's office.*
*She knew the student **who** <u>won the prize.</u>*

The relative pronouns *that* and *which* are used when referring to **objects** as seen in the first example above. (Also see discussion of "WHO | THAT | WHICH" on page 135.)

The other five relative pronouns *who, whom, whose, whoever,* and *whomever* are used when referring to a **person** or **persons** as seen in the second and third examples above. Because of this, they are subject to case considerations and fall into these classifications:

SUBJECT CASE	who, whoever
OBJECT CASE	whom, whomever
POSSESSIVE CASE	whose

The key to determining which of these relative pronouns to use in a sentence is to assess whether the pronoun acts as the subject or object of the dependent clause. Consider this simple sentence.

Judy registered at the county fair.

Now, if you want to tell more about Judy in this sentence using new dependent clauses, you could do so in these ways:

1. With a subject case pronoun:

*Judy, **who** <u>entered the quilt competition</u>, registered at the county fair.*

2. With an object case pronoun:

*Judy, **whom** <u>all of the judges just loved</u>, registered at the county fair.*

3. With a possessive case pronoun:

*Judy, **whose** <u>quilt entry had a good chance of winning</u>, registered at the county fair.*

QUICK TEST:
CORRECT RELATIVE PRONOUN USE

Recall that the relative pronouns **who** and **whoever** are subject pronouns—they perform the action of the verb—and the relative pronouns **whom** and **whomever** are object pronouns—they perform as either direct or indirect objects or objects of the preoposition. To test to see which relative pronoun to use in a dependent clause, substitute a third-person singular pronoun (he/him or she/her) for the relative pronoun, and then assess which sounds correct.

> **EXAMPLE:** *I will always award the prize to (**whoever**, **whomever**) comes in first.*

STEP 1. If a clause, determine how the pronoun functions in the clause, not how the clause serves in the sentence. In this example:

(SUBJECT) *comes in first.*

STEP 2. Substitute a third person singular pronoun:

*(**he/him**) comes in first.*
OR
*(**she/her**) comes in first.*

STEP 3. Determine which sounds correct. In both cases, the subject pronouns sound correct:

he (not him) *comes in first.*
OR
she (not her) *comes in first.*

STEP 4. Select the corresponding relative pronoun. The correct answer is *I will always award the prize to **whoever** comes in first,* because *whoever* is functioning as the subject of the clause and requires a relative pronoun in the subject case.

— DEMONSTRATIVE PRONOUNS —

A **demonstrative pronoun** is one that replaces a noun identified elsewhere in the sentence. There are four different words that commonly serve as demonstrative pronouns:

this   that   (with singular antecedents)
these   those   (with plural antecedents)

*Hand me the papers—**those** on the floor.*
***That** was a terrible disaster, in my opinion.*

— INTERROGATIVE PRONOUNS —

An **interrogative pronoun** is one used to introduce a question (or interrogative sentence). The interrogative pronouns include:

More common: who   whom   whose   what   which
Less common: whoever   whomever   whatever   whichever

***Who** is laughing now?*
***Whomever** would you ask to do that job?*

QUICK TEST: CORRECT INTERROGATIVE
PRONOUN USE IN QUESTIONS

Use who if a question is about the subject and whom when the question is about the object.
To know whether the case is a subject or an object, simply recast the question into a statement
and temporarily substitute the interrogative pronoun with a subject or object pronoun.
Then apply the corresponding subject or object interrogative pronoun.

EXAMPLE: *Who bought the museum tickets?*

STEP 1.   Recast the question into a statement:

I bought the museum tickets.

STEP 2.   *I* is the subject pronoun, so we apply **who**.

EXAMPLE: *Whom does John love?*

STEP 1.   Recast the question into a statement:

*John loves **her**.*

STEP 2.   *Her* is the direct object pronoun so we apply **whom**.

— GUIDELINES FOR PRONOUN USE —

As all of the different types of pronouns identified suggest, some thought often needs to be given to which pronouns are used and how. In addition to principles and practices in the various examples we saw in this chapter, here are some key factors to keep in mind when working with pronouns.

- A pronoun must match the person and number of the noun that it replaces (the pronoun's antecedent). For example, a singular noun calls for a singular pronoun.

Owen plays baseball. He is the starting pitcher.

- A plural noun calls for a plural pronoun.

They needed to start their hike.

- If relevant, a pronoun agrees in gender.

The woman returned to her work.

Note: It is acceptable and becoming more common to use third-person plural pronouns they/them/their (among others) to refer to both singular and plural antecedents so as not to specify gender (see page 52).

Notice in these examples that in order to avoid any confusion or ambiguity: (1) a pronoun needs to refer clearly to one specific antecedent that occurs before the pronoun and (2) a pronoun should be placed relatively close to its antecedent.

- Care should be taken to ensure that the correct pronoun case is used— subject case, object case, or possessive case.

Me and Bobby McGee went to the fair.
(INCORRECT BECAUSE THE PRONOUN SHOULD BE IN THE SUBJECT CASE, SINCE IT IS THE SUBJECT)

Bobby McGee and I went the fair.
(CORRECT)

The salesperson gave Mary and I some free samples.
(INCORRECT BECAUSE THE PRONOUN SHOULD BE IN THE OBJECT CASE, SINCE IT IS THE INDIRECT OBJECT)

The salesperson gave Mary and me some free samples.
(CORRECT)

- Be attentive when using pronouns with **present participles** and **gerunds**. The present participle and the gerund look alike—both are verb forms with the *-ing* ending—but the present participle functions as a verb, and the gerund functions as a noun and requires a possessive pronoun.

*I appreciate **you** making the cake.*

(INCORRECT BECAUSE *MAKING THE CAKE* IS A GERUND PHRASE AND SHOULD BE MODIFIED BY THE POSSESSIVE PRONOUN *YOUR*)

*I appreciate **your** making the cake.*

(CORRECT)

THAN I? OR THAN ME?

The words **than** and **as** are conjunctions used in comparison situations, such as:

*CORRECT: Both of my sons are taller **than I**.*

*INCORRECT: Both of my sons are taller **than me**.*

*CORRECT: My folks are at least as disappointed **as I**.*

*INCORRECT: My folks are at least as disappointed **as me**.*

These examples both indicate that use of the subject pronoun **I** is preferred to the object pronoun **me**. Although it is not immediately evident, the reason is because there is a part in each sentence that is *assumed* and not stated. Using these examples, the fully expressed sentences would be:

*Both of my sons are taller **than I am tall**.*

*My folks are at least as disappointed **as I am disappointed**.*

In these elaborated examples, it should be clear that the pronouns are subjects of the clauses joined by the conjunctions *than* and *as* and therefore require subject pronouns.

HE/SHE OR THEY? OR HIS/HER OR THEIR?

Modern conventions today favor using the third-person plural pronouns they/them/their (among others) to refer to both singular and plural antecedents so as not to specify gender:

*I handed the dropped item to the **person** in line. **They** have it now.*

In situations where the gender of a person is indicated, it is clear which pronoun to use:

***Davis** is the new boy in class. **He** was a little nervous at first. **His** confidence soon returned. **Sarah** is my daughter. **She** lives in California. **Her** house is on the beach.*

But what about when the noun antecedent does not indicate gender, as in:

The student who wants to speak ...

It used to be that not knowing the gender and not wanting to show a gender bias, you would finish the sentence using his or her:

*... needs to raise **his or her** hand.*

That is still correct, but it can often sound awkward, especially if there are multiple occurrences in close context. Today, it is acceptable to use the third person plural form *their*:

*The student who wants to speak needs to raise **their** hand.*

Another approach in this example would be to pluralize it, as in:

***Students** who want to speak need to raise **their** hands.*

CHAPTER 6

FOCUS ON VERBS

Verbs are where the action is. Literally, nothing happens without verbs, whether the happening is an action, an event, a condition, or simply a state of being. Through variations in tense (present, past, future, etc.) verbs also indicate the general time frame in which a happening occurs. In general terms, while the subject of a sentence (that is or contains a noun) identifies who or what is acting or being acted upon, it is the **verb** of a sentence that identifies the nature of the action that occurs. Given this role, the verb is pivotal in expressing meaningful, complete thoughts.

In construction, the verb is also the most complex part of speech, because the form of the verb depends on (1) whether the subject is or is not the speaker of the sentence (**person**), (2) whether the subject is singular or plural (**number**), and (3) when the action of the sentence occurs (**tense**). In addition, verbs express what kinds of attitude are conveyed about the action (**mood**) and if the subject is acting or being acted upon (**voice**). There are numerous verb qualities that are quite useful to know that we will review in this chapter.

― GENERAL TYPES OF VERBS ―

Before getting into the complexities of verb construction, it is useful to understand that at the highest level verbs fall into one of three categories: action verbs, linking verbs, or helping verbs.

ACTION VERBS

An action verb is a word that expresses some form of activity that the subject of the sentence takes. Of the ten thousand or so verbs available for use altogether in the English language, the most by far are action verbs. One important distinction with action verbs is that some take a direct object—as in *Tim **threw** the football*. Others do not—as in *Lauren quietly **meditated***.

LINKING VERBS

A linking verb does *not* show any action but rather renames the subject. It "links" or connects the subject and subject complement (a predicate nominative or predicate adjective) that renames the subject—as in *John* **is** *a student*. The most common linking verb is the verb TO BE and its forms (*am, are, is, was, were, etc.*). Linking verbs also convey senses such as TO FEEL, TO LOOK, TO SMELL, TO SOUND, and TO TASTE. In addition, linking verbs also convey states of being, such as TO APPEAR, TO BECOME, TO GET, TO GROW, TO PROVE, TO REMAIN, TO SEEM, TO STAY, and TO TURN.

> *Whitney* **is** *an excellent STEM teacher.*
> *The old rope bridge* **seems** *really unstable.*
> *Adam* **became** *an emergency room physician.*

LINKING VERBS AND SUBJECT PRONOUNS

As we saw in chapter 5, linking verbs require **subject pronouns** to be used:

The man in the blue coat **was I**.

It **was he** *who bought the museum tickets.*

HELPING VERBS (AKA AUXILIARY VERBS)

There are a number of helping verbs in English that assist in forming the tenses of other verbs, which we will see later in this chapter, such as the present and past perfect, future, and conditional. A helping verb accompanies a form of the main verb to create a **verb phrase**. The three primary helping verbs are TO BE, TO HAVE, and TO DO. When the verb TO BE works as a linking verb, it becomes the main/action verb and not a helping verb. The helping verbs TO HAVE and TO DO can also serve as action verbs.

*John **was** <u>promoted</u> to Lieutenant Commander.*
(PAST PREFECT VERB PHRASE WITH HELPING VERB TO BE)
*Nathan **has** <u>cycled</u> all over Europe.*
(PRESENT PERFECT VERB PHRASE WITH HELPING VERB TO HAVE)

MODAL VERBS

In addition to the three helping verbs TO BE, TO HAVE, and TO DO, there is a special set of verbs called **modal verbs** that help express things that are possible, likely, or allowed. See a more complete description of modal verbs on page 73.

*They **might** get concert tickets.*

— VERB FORMS IN RELATION — TO PERSON AND NUMBER

In order to step into the complexity of verbs, let's start out by focusing in on just one verb—an action verb that expresses an action we all engage in every day— eating! First of all, we generally refer to a verb in its **infinitive** form—TO EAT. Note that the infinitive form combines the preposition *to* with the base of the verb *eat* to create the infinitive TO EAT. Secondly, it is important to know that a verb will take on different **verb forms** that add an ending to its base (*walking, walks, walked*) and sometimes with different spellings (*eating, eats, ate*) that depend on a number of factors.

A grammatically correct verb form will depend on person, number, and tense. Like pronouns in chapter 5, there are three **person** types, and each has a singular and plural form, or **number**. The person types are referred to with the ordinal numbers—first, second, and third, as follows:

First Person: refers to the speaker(s) in the sentence
I (SINGULAR), we (PLURAL)

Second Person: refers to the person(s) spoken to
you (SINGULAR, PLURAL)

Third Person: refers to the person(s) spoken about
he, she, it (SINGULAR), they (PLURAL)

SUBJECT PRONOUNS		
PERSON	**NUMBER**	
	SINGULAR	*PLURAL*
First Person	I	we
Second Person	you	you
Third Person	he, she, it	they

The good news is that English verbs, in comparison to other languages, are pretty straightforward. As you can see in our example below, the only time English verbs change form is in the third-person singular present tense, in which we add an "s" to the verb (*eats*). We will look at why this happens more closely later in the chapter when we look at verb conjugations .

TO EAT (PRESENT TENSE)		
PERSON	*SINGULAR*	*PLURAL*
First Person	I eat	we eat
Second Person	you eat	you eat
Third Person	he, she, it eats	they eat

— SUBJECT/VERB AGREEMENT —

The verb of a sentence *must* agree in number (singular or plural) and person (first, second, or third) with the subject. The subject can be singular (*pear*) or plural (*pears*). It can be first person (*I, we*), second person (*you*), or third person (*he, she, it, they*). Let's look quickly at the irregular verb TO BE to illustrate how number and person work together in terms of verb use. Here are the forms of TO BE that we use to describe things in the present tense.

TO BE (PRESENT TENSE)		
PERSON	*SINGULAR*	*PLURAL*
First Person	I am	we are
Second Person	you are	you are
Third Person	he, she, it is	they are

If you were writing on the subject of a single woman, you would use— *She is a good chess player.* Similarly, if you were writing about a group that includes yourself, you would use—*We are so happy to be here.* Be aware that these shifts in verb form depend on number and person. Failure to make the right match—as in **You is** *a good chess player*—would stand out to others as an obvious grammar error. If the concept of subject/verb agreement does not come easily to you, spend more time on understanding verb conjugations (see page 64-68), where the various forms of number/person verb agreement are illustrated in detail.

TRANSITIVE VERSUS INTRANSITIVE VERBS

An action verb can be transitive or intransitive. A **transitive verb** requires a direct object in order to complete the thought as intended.

*Emily carried an **umbrella**.*

In this sentence, *carried* is a transitive verb and *umbrella* is the direct object. Clearly, the fragment *Emily carried*, without the direct object *umbrella*, does not make sense.

An **intransitive verb** is also an action verb but *without* a direct object:

Emily coughed.

Some verbs can be transitive and intransitive, depending on the other words involved in the sentence. Compare these similar sentences:

*Pete sings a birthday **song**.*
(TRANSITIVE)

Pete sings.
(INTRANSITIVE)

One of the key reasons why it is useful to understand whether a verb requires a direct object or not is that it helps avoid situations of misuse. Consider the verbs TO LAY and TO LIE, for example.

TO LIE, as in *to recline*, is intransitive, as in:

*She planned to **lie** on the bed.*

TO LAY is transitive because it requires a direct object, as in:

*Hens **lay** eggs.*

Knowing this will help avoid the situation of saying: *I'm going to lay down*, which suggests something quite different from saying: *I'm going to **lie** down*.

Similar verb pairs with transitive and intransitive differences include TO SIT / TO SET (see page 133).

– VERB TENSES –

For effective communication, the format of a verb must correctly describe the time period in which the action of the sentence is occurring. It is the **tense** of the verb that makes this happen. Every verb has a total of **twelve tenses** representing three time periods (present, past, and future) and each period contains four tense groups (simple, progressive, perfect, and perfect progressive) that add more nuisance and description to when a verb's event occurs within the present, past, or future time periods. Let's first take a look at a snapshot of all the twelve tenses before we delve into each one individually. Using the third-person singular subject (*she*) and the verb TO WALK, the general framework of the verb tenses is depicted as follows.

TIME PERIOD	SIMPLE TENSES	COMPOUND TENSES		
		PROGRESSIVE	*PERFECT*	*PERFECT PROGRESSIVE*
PRESENT	She walks	She is walking	She has walked	She has been walking
PAST	She walked	She was walking	She had walked	She had been walking
FUTURE	She will walk	She will be walking	She will have walked	She will have been walking

– VERB CONJUGATIONS –

As noted, and for the sake of simplicity, the above table only shows the forms for the third-person singular subject (she) and the main verb tenses. However, if we want to see every form of the verb TO WALK that is possible in the English language, all three persons in the singular and plural would need to be added. Such a complete compilation of all these various forms is called a **verb conjugation**.

When we add verb participles like -ed, -en, or -ing to the base of a verb or add helping verbs such as TO BE or TO HAVE before a verb, we are conjugating the verb so that it conveys the time frame of when the action is happening.

For example, the sentences below all use the verb TO WALK, but the different verb conjugations place the action of "walking" within different time frames (tenses).

John **will walk** *to the store tomorrow.*
(SIMPLE FUTURE TENSE)

John **had walked** *to the store before he* **walked** *the dog.*
(PAST PERFECT TENSE + SIMPLE PAST TENSE)

John **is walking** *now.*
(PRESENT PROGRESSIVE TENSE)

To learn how to correctly conjugate verbs, there are a couple of items we first need to master, such as the role of helping verbs in compound tenses, the key parts of a verb, the difference between regular and irregular verbs, and how to find the base of a verb.

HELPING VERBS

It is especially important to develop a command of the helping verbs TO BE and TO HAVE given their role is creating compound tenses. On the next page are the present, past, and future conjugations of the helping verbs TO BE and TO HAVE.

TO BE			
	PERSON	*SINGULAR*	*PLURAL*
PRESENT	First	I am	we are
	Second	you are	you are
	Third	he, she, it is	they are
PAST	First	I was	we were
	Second	you were	you were
	Third	he, she, it was	they were
FUTURE	First	I will be	we will be
	Second	you will be	you will be
	Third	he, she, it will be	they will be

TO HAVE			
	PERSON	*SINGULAR*	*PLURAL*
PRESENT	First	I have	we have
	Second	you have	you have
	Third	he, she, it has	they have
PAST	First	I had	we had
	Second	you had	you had
	Third	he, she, it had	they had
FUTURE	First	I will have	we will have
	Second	you will have	you will have
	Third	he, she, it will have	they will have

PHRASAL VERBS WITH PARTICLES

Some verbs are linked with a particle to create a verb phrase, such as *give **up***, *break **away***, or
*flip **out***. These are examples of **particles** (bolded in the examples) which are words that add no
distinct meaning in and of themselves, but combine with a verb to create a new verb expressed
in a phrasal form.

VERB FORMS AND PARTICIPLES

In addition to helping verbs, we need to know the key **verb forms** and **participles**
of a main verb to create a verb's complete conjugation. They include the:
(1) infinitive; (2) verb base (or simple form); (3) present tense; (4) third-person
singular present tense (or –s form); (5) past tense; (6) present participle
(or –*ing* form); and (7) past participle. Let's look at the regular verb TO WALK
to see how they are formed.

PRINCIPLE VERB FORMS AND PARTICIPLES FOR "TO WALK"	
The **infinitive**	to walk
Dropping the *to* from the infinitive gives the **verb base** (or simple form).	walk
The verb's **present tense** is the verb base.	walk
The **third-person singular** present tense (or **–s form**) is formed by adding the endings –s or –es to the verb base.	walks
The **past tense** is formed by adding the endings –*d* or –*ed* to the verb base for regular verbs. Irregular verbs have a different past tense form.	walked
The **present participle** is formed by adding the ending –*ing* to the verb base. The present participle (or –***ing* form**) is always accompanied with a helping verb.	walking
The **past participle** for regular verbs is the same form as their past tense (adding an –*d* or –*ed* to the verb base). For irregular verbs, it is formed by either adding an –*en*, -*n*, to the verb base or a complete spelling change. The past participle is always accompanied with a helping verb.	walked

REGULAR AND IRREGULAR VERBS

In conjugating verbs, there is a distinction between regular and irregular verbs. **Regular verbs** follow a standard conjugation pattern. **Irregular verbs** do not. This means that extra work is required to learn the irregular verbs because their conjugations have unusual elements. Unfortunately, there are many irregular verbs in everyday use. Let's look first at regular verbs which do not change forms.

REGULAR VERBS

There is no magic rule to remembering what are regular verbs. As we just learned, the past tense and past participle of regular verbs are the same; we add either *-d* or *-ed* to the verb base. Some examples include:

VERB BASE	PAST TENSE	PAST PARTICIPLE
ask	asked	asked
call	called	called
look	looked	looked
walk	walked	walked

Like so many things, this skill is developed over time with repeated use. As a helpful resource, however, appendix B includes a list of over seven hundred regular verbs presented in alphabetical order to facilitate easy reference.

SPELLING CHANGES FOR SOME REGULAR VERB FORMS

There may be some adjustments that need to be made to some regular verbs depending on their spelling. For example:

If the verb ends in a **consonant + e**	→	chase
Add **-d** to form the past tense and past participle	→	chased
Drop the **-e** and add **-ing** to form the present participle	→	chasing
If the verb ends in a **consonant + y**	→	hurry
Drop the **-y** and add **-ies** to form the third-person singular present tense	→	he/she/it hurries
Drop the **-y** and add **-ied** to form the past tense and past participle	→	hurried
If the verb ends in an **-s** or an **-s** sound	→	buzz
Add **-es** to form the third-person singular present tense (instead of just -s)	→	he/she/it buzzes
If the verb ends in a short **vowel + consonant**	→	wrap
Double the final consonant and add **-ed** to form the past tense and past participle	→	wrapped
Double the final consonant and add **-ing** to form the present participle	→	wrapping

CONJUGATION TEMPLATE FOR REGULAR VERBS

Let's look at our verb example TO WALK again to see how the endings are applied to the verb's base *walk*. The chart serves as a complete conjugation template for regular verbs and shows all of the verb forms of the various tenses including the subject's number and person.

INFINITIVE TO WALK	VERB BASE	walk	
	PAST TENSE	walk + ed	
	PRESENT PARTICIPLE	walk + ing	
	PAST PARTICIPLE	walk + ed	
	PERSON	**SINGULAR**	**PLURAL**
PRESENT	First	I **walk**	we **walk**
	Second	you **walk**	you **walk**
	Third	he, she, it **walk** + s	they **walk**
PAST	All	I, we, you, he, she, it, they **walk** + ed	
FUTURE	All	I, we, you, he, she, it, they **will walk**	
PRESENT PROGRESSIVE (PRESENT TENSE OF BE + PRESENT PARTICIPLE)	First	I **am walk** + ing	we **are walk** + ing
	Second	you **are walk** + ing	you **are walk** + ing
	Third	he, she, it **is walk** + ing	they **are walk** + ing
PAST PROGRESSIVE (PAST TENSE OF BE + PRESENT PARTICIPLE)	First	I **was walk** + ing	we **were walk** + ing
	Second	you **were walk** + ing	you **were walk** + ing
	Third	he, she, it **was walk** + ing	they **were walk** + ing
FUTURE PROGRESSIVE (FUTURE TENSE OF BE + PRESENT PARTICIPLE)	All	I, we, you, he, she, it, they **will be walk** + ing	
PRESENT PERFECT (PRESENT TENSE OF HAVE + PAST PARTICIPLE)	First	I **have walk** + ed	we **have walk** + ed
	Second	you **have walk** + ed	you **have walk** + ed
	Third	he, she, it **has walk** + ed	they **have walk** + ed
PAST PERFECT (PAST TENSE OF HAVE + PAST PARTICIPLE)	All	I, we, you, he, she, it, they **had walk** + ed	
FUTURE PERFECT (FUTURE TENSE OF HAVE + PAST PARTICIPLE)	All	I, we, you, he, she, it, they **will have walk** + ed	

		I	we
PRESENT PERFECT PROGRESSIVE (PRESENT PERFECT TENSE OF BE + PRESENT PARTICIPLE)	First	**have been walk** + ing	**have been walk** + ing
	Second	you **have been walk** + ing	you **have been walk** + ing
	Third	he, she, it **has been walk** + ing	they **have been walk** + ing
PAST PERFECT PROGRESSIVE (PAST PERFECT TENSE OF BE + PRESENT PARTICIPLE)	All	I, we, you, he, she, it, they **had been walk** + ing	
FUTURE PERFECT PROGRESSIVE (FUTURE PERFECT TENSE OF BE + PRESENT PARTICIPLE)	All	I, we, you, he, she, it, they **will have been walk** + ing	

IRREGULAR VERBS

Unfortunately, the shortcuts to create regular verb forms are not available for irregular verbs, which contain spelling changes in the past tense and past participle that regular verbs do not. Some examples include:

VERB BASE	PAST TENSE	PAST PARTICIPLE
become	became	become
begin	began	begun
bring	brought	brought
draw	drew	drawn
go	went	gone
give	gave	given
grow	grew	grown
see	saw	seen
speak	spoke	spoken
take	took	taken

Again, proficiency will come with time and use. In appendix B there are a few aids for irregular verbs available, including full conjugations for the three primary helping verbs (TO BE, TO HAVE, and TO DO) and the key verb forms for more than 150 irregular verbs, with some of the most common irregular verbs shown separately.

CONJUGATION TEMPLATE FOR IRREGULAR VERBS

Let's look at the complete conjugation table for the irregular verb TO EAT. Notice the past tense is irregular (*ate*) and the past participle is also irregular (*eaten*).

VERB INFINITIVE	VERB BASE	eat	
	PAST TENSE	ate	
TO EAT	PRESENT PARTICIPLE	eating	
	PAST PARTICIPLE	eaten	
	PERSON	SINGULAR	PLURAL
PRESENT	First	I eat	we eat
	Second	you eat	you eat
	Third	he, she, it eats	they eat
PAST	All	I, we, you, he, she, it, they ate	
FUTURE	All	I, we, you, he, she, it, they will eat	
PRESENT PROGRESSIVE (PRESENT TENSE OF BE + PRESENT PARTICIPLE)	First	I am eating	we are eating
	Second	you are eating	you are eating
	Third	he, she, it is eating	they are eating
PAST PROGRESSIVE (PAST TENSE OF BE + PRESENT PARTICIPLE)	First	I was eating	we were eating
	Second	you were eating	you were eating
	Third	he, she, it was eating	they were eating
FUTURE PROGRESSIVE (FUTURE TENSE OF BE + PRESENT PARTICIPLE)	All	I, we, you, he, she, it, they will be eating	

PRESENT PERFECT	First	I have eaten	we have eaten
(PRESENT TENSE OF HAVE + PAST PARTICIPLE)	Second	you have eaten	you have eaten
	Third	he, she, it has eaten	they have eaten
PAST PERFECT (PAST TENSE OF HAVE + PAST PARTICIPLE)	All	I, we, you, he, she, it, they had eaten	
FUTURE PERFECT (FUTURE TENSE OF HAVE + PAST PARTICIPLE)	All	I, we, you, he, she, it, they will have eaten	
PRESENT PERFECT PROGRESSIVE	First	I have been eating	we have been eating
(PRESENT PERFECT TENSE OF BE + PRESENT PARTICIPLE)	Second	you have been eating	you have been eating
	Third	he, she, it has been eating	they have been eating
PAST PERFECT PROGRESSIVE (PAST PERFECT TENSE OF BE + PRESENT PARTICIPLE)	All	I, we, you, he, she, it, they had been eating	
FUTURE PERFECT PROGRESSIVE (FUTURE PERFECT TENSE OF BE + PRESENT PARTICIPLE)	All	I, we, you, he, she, it, they will have been eating	

- A CLOSER LOOK AT VERB TENSES -

Now that we have looked at how to conjugate verbs, let's take a closer look at the different tenses the conjugations convey and how they are formed. First, we must look at the differences among simple, perfect, and progressive tenses.

Simple tenses place the action of the verb into the present, past (aka **preterit**), and future. The present conveys what is ocurring now. The past describes an event that already occurred. The future is an event that has not yet happened.

Ben **speaks** highly of his supervisor.
(SIMPLE PRESENT)

Sally **ate** the apple.
(SIMPLE PAST)

George **will go** to the movie theater tomorrow night.
(SIMPLE FUTURE, ALSO A COMPOUND TENSE)

Compound tenses consist of two or more words (*I have spoken*). In addition to the simple future tense above, the following tenses are all compound tenses.

Perfect tenses are compound verb tenses consisting of (1) a form of the helping verb TO HAVE and (2) the main verb's past participle (*have walked*, *had traveled*, *will have eaten*). The perfect tenses add a bit more detail about the verb's action than the simple past tense and usually describe events that have been finished, or will be finished, before a more recent event.

John **has been** to Italy before.
(PRESENT PERFECT = THE ACTION STARTED AND FINISHED IN THE PAST
BUT IS STILL FELT IN THE PRESENT)

Sally **had eaten** before she arrived to the party.
(PAST PERFECT = THE ACTION FINISHED BEFORE ANOTHER ACTION TOOK PLACE)

The team **will have practiced** a lot before the competition.
(FUTURE PERFECT = THE ACTION WILL FINISH BEFORE A SPECIFIC TIME)

Progressive tenses are compound verb tenses formed with two or more words that contain (1) one form of the helping verb TO BE and (2) the present participle (*-ing* form) of the action verb (*has been reading, had been listening, will have been working*). The progressive tenses show that the action of the verb is continuous and does not have a specific end.

George **is practicing** the piano.
(PRESENT PROGRESSIVE = THE EVENT IS TAKING PLACE NOW)

The concession stand **was selling** tons of ice cream cones.
(PAST PROGRESSIVE = INDICATES AN ONGOING NATURE OF A PAST ACTION)

Because Erin **is traveling** tomorrow, she needs to start packing quickly.
(FUTURE PROGRESSIVE = THE ACTION WILL CONTINUE TO OCCUR FOR A WHILE)

Perfect Progressive tenses are compound verb tenses formed with (1) one form of the helping verb TO BE and (2) the present participle (*-ing* form) of the action verb (*has been listening, had been walking, will have been jogging*). The perfect progressive tenses show a continuous action in the past that will continue.

The group **has been waiting** for over thirty minutes.
(PRESENT PERFECT PROGRESSIVE = DESCRIBES AN OCCURRING EVENT
IN THE PAST THAT WILL CONTINUE)

We **had been rehearsing** the scene before Jill entered the stage.
(PAST PERFECT PROGRESSIVE = DESCRIBES AN OCCURRING ACTION IN THE PAST
THAT ENDED BEFORE A SECOND ACTION)

We **will have been working** on the report for three days by the time they present it.
(FUTURE PERFECT PROGRESSIVE = AN ACTION THAT WILL CONTINUE)

— QUICK VERB TENSE REVIEW —

To recap all of the verb tenses in convenient charts, here are the present, past, and future tenses using the irregular verb TO EAT in all tenses with short descriptions of each.

PRESENT TENSES			
SIMPLE PRESENT	PRESENT PROGRESSIVE	PRESENT PERFECT	PRESENT PERFECT PROGRESSIVE
A girl **eats** the pie.	A girl **is eating** the pie.	A girl **has eaten** the pie.	A girl **has been eating** the pie.
	Present Tense of TO BE (am, are, is) plus Present Participle	Present Tense of TO HAVE (have, has) plus Past Participle	Present Perfect Tense of TO BE (have been, has been) plus Present Participle
A simple tense used to express an action or event occurring in the present time.	A compound tense used to express a continuous action or event at the present time.	A compound tense used to express a past action or event without reference to a specific time.	A compound tense used to express a continuous action either completed or initiated in the past.

PAST TENSES			
SIMPLE PAST	**PAST PROGRESSIVE**	**PAST PERFECT**	**PAST PERFECT PROGRESSIVE**
*A girl **ate** the pie.*	*A girl **was eating** the pie.*	*A girl **had eaten** the pie.*	*A girl **had been eating** the pie.*
	Past Tense of TO BE (was, were) **plus Present Participle**	**Past Tense of TO HAVE** (had) **plus Past Participle**	**Past Perfect Tense of TO BE** (had been) **plus Present Participle**
A simple tense used to express a past action or event.	A compound tense used to express a continuous action or event at a time in the past.	A compound tense used to express a past action or event completed before another past action or event.	A compound tense used to express a continuous action or event completed at some point in the past.

FUTURE TENSES			
SIMPLE FUTURE	**FUTURE PROGRESSIVE**	**FUTURE PERFECT**	**FUTURE PERFECT PROGRESSIVE**
*A girl **will eat** the pie.*	*A girl **will be eating** the pie.*	*A girl **will have eaten** the pie.*	*A girl **will have been eating** the pie.*
	Future Tense of TO BE (will be) **plus Present Participle**	**Future Tense of TO HAVE** (will have) **plus Past Participle**	**Future Perfect Tense of TO BE** (will have been) **plus Present Participle**
A simple tense used to express an action or event that will occur at a time in the future.	A compound tense used to express a continuous action or event at a time in the future.	A compound tense used to express a future action or event completed before another future action or event.	A compound tense used to express a continuous action or event that will be completed at some point in the future.

— OTHER IMPORTANT VERB ATTRIBUTES —

In addition to tenses, which specify the time period in which the action of the verb is occurring, verbs are critical in establishing three other important verb qualities—modality, voice, and mood.

MODALITY

There is a set of verbs whose role is to define the extent to which the action being expressed is possible, probable, likely, or permitted. They are called the **modal verbs**, and there are ten of them:

can   could   will   would   shall   should

may   might   must   ought (to)

- We use modal verbs as a form of helping verbs with the base form of another verb to address such situations as:

Possibility:	*She **might go** to her friend's house.*
Certainty:	*They **will take** the tent down in the morning.*
Necessity:	*We **must finish** this project tonight!*

- Modal verbs are not used on their own. When converting a modal statement to **a modal question**, simply move the subject between the two verbs.

  Must <u>we</u> finish this project tonight?

- Modal verbs *do not* have tenses, but a **past modal** construction can be created by using MODAL VERB + HAVE + PAST PARTICIPLE of the main verb.

  *I **should have done** it yesterday.*

VOICE

The main verb in a sentence should be constructed to "speak" in a desired voice, which is either an active voice or a passive voice. The word *voice* in grammar tells us about the subject of the sentence. It answers the question, Does the subject perform or receive the action of the verb? When the subject is *performing* the action, it is called the **active voice** and is the most common construction, typically following the format SUBJECT + VERB + OBJECT.

*The manager **printed** the confidential report.*

When the subject is *receiving* the action, it is called the **passive voice** and is created by an appropriate form of the verb TO BE + PAST PARTICIPLE of the main verb. The sentence above recast in the passive voice would be:

*The confidential report **was printed** by the manager.*

In many situations, the passive voice is seen as a weaker, more indirect way to present information, and the active voice is often favored when writing. However, there are times where the passive voice makes more sense, such as when the performer of the action is not important as in:

*The estate sale sign **will be posted** on Wednesday.*

ACTIVE VOICE VERSUS PASSIVE VOICE

Even though grammar instructors encourage the use of the active voice, the passive voice is preferred in situations where you want to emphasize the *receiver* of the action as opposed to the *performer* of the action. In this example, what passed is more important than who did the passing.

*The Civil Rights Act **was passed** in 1964.*

MOOD

The format of a verb also conveys the proper **mood** of the sentence, which in effect makes clear what kind of sentence is being stated: Is it a statement, a command, a hypothetical situation, a question, or a conditional situation? In grammar, the word *mood* does not mean the same as when we refer to someone's current mood. Instead, it is more similar in context to the word *situation*. So, when we say that there are **five moods** that verbs can express, we are suggesting that the moods describe the five different situations that verbs can create, such as a conditional situation, a command situation, etc. The five moods that verbs can express include:

(1) **Indicative mood** is used in statements of fact formed with the standard conjugated verb forms.

> He **will arrive** tomorrow.
> The dog **chased** its tail.

(2) **Imperative mood** is used in commands and instructions, formed by the verb base positioned usually at the beginning of the sentence.

> **Listen** to me.

A negative imperative is formed using *do not* before the verb base.

> **Do not listen** to me.

THE SUBJUNCTIVE MOOD

The subjunctive mood is not as significant in modern-day English. Learning to use it is not intuitive, and usage of the subjunctive mood often sounds awkward and stilted. One common workaround strategy is to replace a verb in the subjunctive mood—as in *It is best **that she leave** her current employer*—with the infinitive form—as in *It is best **for her to leave** her current employer.*

(3) **Subjunctive mood** is used in hypothetical situations (with such words as *if, unless, wish*) and formed using *were* (the third-person past tense of TO BE).

> *If I **were** rich, I would buy a mansion.*
> *I wish this activity **were** over.*

(4) **Interrogative mood** is used in questions and is formed using a helping verb and a form of the main verb, usually in this sequence.

> ***Did** she **leave** a key?*
> ***Are** you **going** to the movies?*

(5) **Conditional mood** is used in requests and situations involving a dependency on something else, and is formed by integrating the helping verbs *would* or *should.*

> *I **would** like a sandwich if it's easy to make.*
> *I **would** ride to your house if it doesn't get too late.*
> *I **would** have gone to the party if I felt better.*
> *I **should** have gone to the meeting.*

$-$ VERB PHRASES $-$

There are several common types of **verb phrases** that are created with verb forms but serve as other parts of speech that include the following:

(1) An **infinitive phrase** is a combination of words that starts with the infinitive of a verb and functions as a noun.

> *To learn is one of the greatest human capabilities.*

(2) A **gerund phrase** is a combination of words that starts with a gerund, which is the *-ing* form of a verb, and functions as a noun.

> *Wiping the slate clean is important to do from time to time.*

(3) A **participle phrase** is a combination of words that starts with the present participle or past participle of a verb and always functions as an adjective.

> *The bee seeking nectar found a "gold mine" in the flower garden.*

CHAPTER 7

FOCUS ON ADVERBS

Adverbs are the companions of verbs. These words can often be quite dramatic in describing a variety of circumstances associated with a verb's action—as in *Her heart beat **wildly***. Adverbs work with verbs, adjectives, and other adverbs to elaborate on the concept being expressed. For example, consider this sentence:

*A cheetah runs **fast**.*

The word *fast* is an adverb and, without it, the complete thought is that *A cheetah runs*. The addition of the adverb *fast* enhances meaning with more information on how the cheetah runs. As seen, single words can function as adverbs as well as word phrases. Typically, adverbs (and adverb phrases) answer the following questions:

How?	*She ran **quickly**.*
When?	*We will finish our report **tomorrow**.*
Where?	*The neighborhood kids usually played **there**.*
Why?	*The pianist played **for extra money**.*
How often?	*He got the newspaper **daily**.*
How long?	*The young lovers embraced **briefly**.*
How much?	*She ate her peas **completely**.*
To what extent?	*The teen studied **enough** to pass.*

The above examples all show adverbs modifying verbs, but adverbs can also modify an **adjective**, another **adverb**, a **preposition**, or a **clause**, as illustrated on the next page.

Adverb modifying an **adjective**:	*The poster was **highly** objectionable.* (How objectionable? **Highly** objectionable.)
Adverb modifying an **adverb**:	*The baby cried **very** loudly.* (How loudly? **Very** loudly)
Adverb modifying a **preposition**:	*The plane is **just** below the horizon.* (How much below? **Just** below.)
Adverb modifying a **clause**:	***Unfortunately**, the program was cancelled.* (Expresses a feeling about the sentence in general.)

There is no one form of an adverb, and there is no master list. Generally, adverbs are identified within the context of the sentence by assessing what question is being answered (see previous page). There are, however, some tips that help in mastering the identification and use of adverbs:

- Many adverbs end in **-ly** and, in many of those cases, the adverb is formed by adding *-ly* to the adjective counterpart, as in:

bad → ***badly***		*colorful* → *colorfully*.	
ADJECTIVE	ADVERB	ADJECTIVE	ADVERB

- Adverbs that are commonly used with **other adverbs** include:

almost   somewhat   quite   often   only   very   too

- Adverbs that are commonly used with **clauses/sentences** include:

accordingly   fortunately/unfortunately   generally   happily/unhappily

hopefully   interestingly   quickly

QUICK TEST: HOW TO IDENTIFY AN ADVERB IN A SENTENCE

Use this quick test to easily identify an adverb in a sentence.

STEP 1. Determine the word or phrase that is described/modified/informed (target).

*The black stallion in Lane 3 <u>raced</u> **quickly** down the stretch.*

STEP 2. Ask: *Is the target a verb, an adjective, or another adverb?*

IF NO = MODIFIER IS NOT AN ADVERB.

IF YES = MODIFIER IS PROBABLY AN ADVERB, proceed.

STEP 3. Ask: *Does the word in question answer any of the questions: How? When? Where? Why? How often? How long? How much? To what extent?*

IF NO = MODIFIER IS NOT AN ADVERB

IF YES = MODIFIER IS PROBABLY AN ADVERB.

Raced how? ***Quickly****.*

– CLAUSE-BASED ADVERBS –

In addition to single words and short phrases serving as adverbs (as illustrated in the previous examples), there are some situations where an entire clause serves in an adverbial capacity.

ADVERB CLAUSES

An **adverb clause** is a dependent clause in which the entire clause serves as an adverb in modifying a verb, an adjective, or another adverb. An adverb clause has a subject and predicate (sometimes one or both might be implied), begins with a **subordinating conjunction** (see page 86 for a full list), and can appear at the beginning of a sentence, in the middle, or at the end as illustrated in these examples:

If you hurry, you will win one of the best door prizes.

Caramel popcorn, although (it is) delicious, is sticky on the fingers.

We'll get started on the trip after I get the car all packed.

CONJUNCTIVE ADVERBS

There is a group of adverbs called **conjunctive adverbs** that connect two independent clauses. A conjunctive adverb introduces one of the independent clauses and makes it dependent and thus modifies the main independent clause. As it does so, the conjunctive adverb identifies the type of the relationship between the clauses. The table below shows the conjunctive adverbs organized by relationship type, along with examples.

RELATIONSHIP	CONJUNCTIVE ADVERB	EXAMPLES
TIME	before, lately, meanwhile, now, since	*Bobbie had to leave **before** dinner was over.*
CAUSE/EFFECT	accordingly, consequently, hence, then, therefore, thus	*Bill retired; **therefore**, he worked on the textbook from his home office.*
ADDITION	additionally, also, finally, first, furthermore, in addition, moreover, next, still, besides	*Matt is a firearm aficionado; **furthermore**, he collects hunting knives.*
COMPARISON	as, like, likewise, similarly	*Ronan lives in Ireland; **likewise**, his sister, Lile, does too.*
CONTRAST	but, still, despite, conversely, otherwise, however, in contrast, in spite of, instead, nevertheless, nonetheless, on the other hand, rather	*Logan seemed very tired; **nevertheless**, he hung in there through dinner.*
EMPHASIS	certainly, definitely, in fact, indeed, of course, undoubtedly	*Doug has a great farm; **in fact**, it is one of the finest in Burlington County.*
SUMMARY OR RESULT	briefly, finally, thus, in conclusion, in summary, merely, quickly, therefore, thus, consequently, then	*Rebecca advanced several arguments in support of social reform; **finally**, she said, "Let's get started."*
ILLUSTRATION	for example, for instance, namely, representatively, typically	*Judy wins quilting competitions regularly; **for example**, she took a top prize last month.*

Note that conjunctive adverbs are used in the connection of two independent clauses. In a situation when there is one independent clause and one dependent clause, there is a set of **subordinating conjunctions** that serve as the connectors, which is treated in more detail in chapter 8.

PUNCTUATION TIP

Use a **semicolon** when a conjunctive adverb falls in the middle of two independent clauses and a comma when they fall elsewhere.

*Sally does not speak Spanish; **however**, she speaks French.*

***However**, Sally does not speak Spanish, but she speaks French.*

*Sally does not speak Spanish but she speaks French, **however**.*

— DETERMINING AN ADVERB AND ADJECTIVE —

Because adjectives and adverbs modify things, they can sometimes appear to be very similar, and it can be difficult to tell which is which. However, their functions are very different. **Adjectives** *only* modify nouns and pronouns (she, we, they, it, etc.). **Adverbs** *only* modify verbs, adjectives, and other adverbs.

*That was a **selfish** attempt to attract attention.*
(SELFISH MODIFIES THE NOUN **ATTEMPT** = ADJECTIVE)

*She was acting **selfishly**.*
(SELFISHLY MODIFIES THE VERB PHRASE **WAS ACTING** = ADVERB)

*Our waiter was **selfishly** arrogant.*
(SELFISHLY MODIFIES THE ADJECTIVE **ARROGANT** = ADVERB)

DOUBLE NEGATIVES

Be careful to not use **double negatives**, which are two negatives in a sentence, such as *barely, hardly, never, no, none, not, nothing,* and *scarcely,* especially when used with contractions.

Sally ***never*** has ***any*** extra time for fun. (CORRECT)

Sally ***never*** has ***no*** extra time for fun. (INCORRECT)

I ***didn't*** understand ***anything*** the speaker said. (CORRECT)

I ***didn't*** understand ***nothing*** the speaker said. (INCORRECT)

BAD VS BADLY

Bad is an adjective and **badly** is an adverb. Usually seen with the linking verbs TO GROW, TO FEEL, and TO TASTE, the adjective bad should be used when the verb is a linking verb.

My coworker <u>felt</u> bad.
(*FELT* IS A LINKING VERB = BAD, ADJECTIVE)

My friend <u>dances</u> badly.
(*DANCES* IS AN ACTION VERB = BADLY, ADVERB)

WELL VS GOOD

Good is always an adjective, no matter what. **Well**, on the other hand, is both an adjective and adverb. When used as an adjective, well *only* refers to health; when it's used to refer to anything else it functions as an adverb.

*Jane is a **good** student.*
(GOOD = ADJECTIVE)

*Robert looks **well**.*
(WELL = ADJECTIVE, DESCRIBING HEALTH)

*That idea doesn't suit him **well**.*
(WELL = ADVERB)

CHAPTER 8

FOCUS ON CONJUNCTIONS, PREPOSITIONS, AND INTERJECTIONS

U p to this point, we have covered the most substantive parts of speech—nouns, adjectives, pronouns, verbs, and adverbs. There remains a category that includes conjunctions, prepositions, and interjections. While these parts of speech do not bring a great deal of meaning, they are tools that are integral to connecting and combining words in many meaningful ways.

— CONJUNCTIONS —

Conjunctions are used to make connections—to connect words, phrases, clauses, and/or sentences. Although there are only a handful of words that serve as the primary conjunctions, there are plenty of others. The three types of conjunctions are:

(1) A **coordinating conjunction** joins elements that are of roughly equal value in a sentence. Coordinating conjunctions are the most frequently used conjunctions, and there are seven words that primarily serve in this way:

and   but   or   nor   for   so   yet

*The dog **and** the cat hid under the sofa together.*
(*AND* CONNECTS THE NOUNS DOG AND CAT)
Neither *Meghan* **nor** *Lucy has visited the new library yet.*
(*NEITHER … NOR* CONNECT THE NOUNS MEGHAN AND LUCY)
*The little girl wanted to go on the ride, **yet** she still had hesitations.*
(*YET* CONNECTS THE TWO INDEPENDENT SENTENCES)

PUNCTUATION TIP

Always use a comma before a coordinating conjunction when it is used to connect two independent clauses.

*My dog is such a good listener, **but** your dog never listens.*

*Tina did not feel like going to the movies, **and** Jeff didn't want to go either.*

(2) A **correlative conjunction** is a word pair that works together to create equal connections. The most common are:

either/or   both/and   neither/nor   not/but   not only/but also

*Either Nemo will eat the cookie, **or** Summer will grab it.*

*Neither his car **nor** his motorcycle was in good working order.*

(3) A **subordinating conjunction** is a word or phrase that *always* introduces a **dependent (or subordinate) adverb clause** to an independent clause and identifies the type of the relationship. The following table shows the subordinating conjunctions organized by relationship type, along with examples.

RELATIONSHIP	SUBORDINATING CONJUNCTION	EXAMPLES
TIME	after, as soon as, as long as, before, by the time, now that, once, since, till, until, when, whenever, while	*By the time Jeff got home, it was too late for dinner.*
CAUSE/EFFECT	as, because, since, so that, in order (that), that	*Patti arranged for a knee replacement **because** the pain became too much to bear.*
COMPARISON	as much as, rather than, than, whereas, whether	***As much as** Rob wanted to travel, the restrictions kept him at home.*
CONCESSION	although, even though, though	*William and CJ both want to go, **although** William is running a slight temperature.*
CONDITION	assuming that, even if, if, in case (that), lest, only if, provided that, unless	*Rebecca will be an excellent researcher, **assuming that** she heads in that direction.*
LOCATION	where, wherever	***Wherever** Christian goes, the other kids want to play with him.*
MANNER	as if, as though, how	*Emma marched into the cafeteria **as if** she were in charge.*

In addition to the above chart, **relative adjectives** and **relative pronouns** can also serve as subordinating conjunctions, as shown here:

RELATIVE ADJECTIVES	whatever, which, whichever	*She would sing either song, **whichever** the group preferred.*
RELATIVE PRONOUNS	who, whoever, whom, whomever, whose	*Lauren promised to help the winner, **whoever** that turned out to be.*

PUNCTUATION TIP

When a sentence begins with a dependent (subordinate) adverb clause, add a comma.

Since we arrived so late to the restaurant, we lost our reservation.

Even though we worked nonstop, we did not make our due date.

– PREPOSITIONS –

Prepositions are words that come before a noun or pronoun to form a prepositional phrase that is itself used to modify a noun, an adverb, or an adjective. *Which woman? The woman in love.* A **preposition** accompanies (and usually precedes) a noun or a pronoun to relate it to some other word in the sentence—a verb, an adjective, or another noun. For example, in the following sentence, the preposition *to* precedes the noun *store* in order to identify where Nannie took the toy:

*Nannie returned the broken toy **to the store**.*

The preposition with the accompanying noun (and other included words) creates what is called a **prepositional phrase**. In our example above, *to the store* is the prepositional phrase. *Store* is the **object of the preposition**. Note that this example creates a relationship of direction. There are other relationships that prepositions help create which include:

Direction:	*Nannie returned the broken toy **to** the store.*
Time:	*The mail usually arrives **before** 11:30.*
Location:	*The principal stood **at** the podium.*
Manner:	*She made her paisley backpack **by** hand.*
Cause/Effect:	*He caught a cold **from** the cold.*
Amount:	*The teacher's starting salary is **over** $30,000.*

PRONOUN CASE
WITH PREPOSITIONAL PHRASES

Because prepositional phrases always have an object, be sure to use **object pronouns** (see page 39) with prepositions. It is most commonly seen with the prepositions *after, between, for, from, to,* and *with.*

*Our team captain agreed <u>with Erin and</u> **me** that we needed a deadline extension.*

*Tina handed the ice cream cone <u>to Jeff and</u> **me**.*

Many prepositions are single words that are referred to as **simple prepositions**, and the most frequently used simple prepositions are:

about	before	into	to
after	between	like	under
against	by	of	with
among	during	on	without
around	for	out	
as	from	over	
at	in	through	

Other prepositions include:

aboard	amid	bar	besides
above	amidst	behind	beyond
across	amongst	below	but
along	astride	beneath	come
alongside	atop	beside	concerning

considering	less	regarding	underneath
counting	minus	respecting	unlike
despite	near	round	until
down	next	save	unto
effective	notwithstanding	saving	up
except	off	short	upon
excepting	onto	since	via
excluding	opposite	than	vice
failing	outside	throughout	within
following	past	till	
including	per	toward	
inside	plus	towards	

Word phrases of two or more words can also function as prepositions. They are called **compound prepositions**, and the following are among those that are most frequently used:

according to	back to	in place of	outside of
across from	based on	in spite of	owing to
adjacent to	because of	inside of	prior to
ahead of	by means of	instead of	pursuant to
along with	close to	left of	rather than
apart from	counter to	near to	regardless of
as far as	down on	next to	right of
as for	due to	on account of	subsequent to
as of	except for	on behalf of	such as
as opposed to	far from	on top of	thanks to
as per	in accordance with	opposite of	up to
as regards	in addition to	opposite to	with regard to
as soon as	in case of	other than	
as well as	in front of	out from	
aside from	in lieu of	out of	

— INTERJECTIONS —

Interjections express strong emotion, such as joy, surprise, anger, or enthusiasm. A word (or phrase) is usually used in isolation in an exclamatory way. **Interjections** are usually one word or a short phrase.

Bravo! You are the new champion.

An interjection is considered a type of sentence (exclamatory) even though it will rarely have a subject or predicate. Many different words or short phrases are used as interjections, and they integrate varying parts of speech. Here is a sampling of the breadth of interjections:

alas	excellent	hello	oh
amen	fabulous	hmm	ouch
baloney	fantastic	indeed	please
bingo	finally	marvelous	welcome
bravo	good grief	my	well
brilliant	ha	no problem	wow
cheers	hallelujah	no way	
duh	heavens	nuts	

PUNCTUATION TIP

Although most interjections use an exclamation point, if they appear within a sentence, use a comma after it.

Oh, I cannot believe she said that!

CHAPTER 9

FOCUS ON PUNCTUATION AND FORMATTING

When you are speaking (as opposed to writing), there is not much opportunity to use punctuation, although "air quotes" are sometimes used via hand gestures. Similarly, with capitalization and format tools (*italics*, underlining, etc.), you cannot use the appearance of words to make or reinforce a point, since there are no words visible. In writing, however, these pieces are integral partners to the words on the page to create and communicate meaning.

A set of marks is available to influence the visual appearance of the words that are used to create meaning, and the marks themselves become important elements of our message. An often-cited example is the statement: *Let's eat, Grandpa*. Without the comma, the statement becomes: *Let's eat Grandpa*, and a new meaning is created. The punctuation marks used most frequently are the following sixteen signs, or sign combinations, which are followed by some key points to keep in mind when using them.

.	period	;	semicolon
,	comma	-	hyphen
?	question mark	–	en dash
!	exclamation point	—	em dash
'	apostrophe	( )	parentheses
" "	quotation marks	[ ]	brackets
' '	single quotation marks	. . .	ellipsis
:	colon	(/) (\)	forward and backward slash

PERIOD

A period is used:

- at the end of a sentence (unless the sentence is ended by a question mark, an exclamation point, or an ellipsis)

  Angela led the session on building resilience.

- at the end of an abbreviation

  February = Feb.
  Doctor = Dr.
  United States = U.S.
  Illinois = IL.

  (**Note**: *It's also common to see state abbreviations without periods, which is also correct.*)

- as a decimal in numerical expressions

  Drew lives exactly 6.9 miles from campus.

- outside a parenthetical aside that comes at the end of a sentence

  Linda loves Ted (the puppy).

- inside a parenthetical aside that is a stand-alone sentence

  Linda loves Ted. (But Robert gets night duty.)

- inside ending quotation marks (single or double)

  Julie wrote, "Montclair really is the Brooklyn of New Jersey."

COMMA

A comma is used:

- before coordinating conjunctions when connecting two independent clauses

    They moved to California, and they never left the state again.

- after introductory words, phrases, and clauses

    In an emergency, the EMTs will report to work when called.

- to separate two or more adjectives describing the same noun

    The long-distance runner took a long, steady drink from his water bottle.

- to set off words, phrases, and clauses in the middle of a sentence that are nonessential to the meaning of the sentence

    A German Shorthair Pointer, my personal favorite, won best of show.
    John, who is a farmer, works a lot.
    The green car, which is my favorite, is very expensive.

- to separate three or more items in a list

    The customer asked for sliced ham, a pound of cheese, and two pickles.

    (Note: See the "Oxford Comma" box on page 94.)

- Do not use a comma with essential phrases and clauses

    The car that is green is my favorite.
    (ESSENTIAL PHRASE = SPECIFIES A PARTICULAR CAR)
    The new computers working with the latest updates are fast.
    (ESSENTIAL PHRASE = SPECIFIES WHICH COMPUTERS)

- in transitions between main text and quoted text

    "Noise pollution can be a problem," Julie wrote.

- to identify quotes

    He said, "I do not want to go ice skating."

- to set off certain items in a sentence, including:

    · **Dates:** *He was born on October 27, 2019, at 11:55 p.m.*

    · **Titles:** *The speech by C. Everett Koop, M.D., was controversial.*

    · **Addresses:** *The show emanated from:*
    30 Rockefeller Center, Eighth Floor
    New York, New York.

    · **Geographic Jurisdications:** *They traveled from Swarthmore, Pennsylvania,*
    to San Francisco, California.

    · **Informal Correspondence:** *Dear Sally,*

THE "OXFORD COMMA" (AKA "SERIAL COMMA")

There is a difference of opinion in the grammar world regarding the serial comma that is used to separate a list of three or more items. The traditional practice, established by Oxford University Press, is to include a comma before the conjunction in a series:

the red, white, and blue flag

A common practice is to omit that last comma:

the red, white and blue flag

Given the options, whichever method is chosen should be used consistently.

QUESTION MARK

A question mark is used:

* at the end of a question (an interrogative sentence)

Is that all there is?

Never use a question mark with periods, commas, or exclamation points:

He yelled out, "Is that all there is?"
(CORRECT)
He yelled out, "Is that all there is?!"
(INCORRECT)

EXCLAMATION POINT

An exclamation point, also referred to as an exclamation mark, is used:

* at the end of an exclamation or interjection to indicate emphasis, volume, or high emotion

I really mean it!

Never use a exclamation point with periods, commas, or question marks:

"I really mean it!" he shouted.
(CORRECT)
"I really mean it!," he shouted.
(INCORRECT)

APOSTROPHE

An apostrophe is used:

* to show possession for singular and plural nouns

That is Susan's car.
(SINGULAR NOUN)
The girls' party.
(PLURAL NOUN)

- to show the omission of letters with contractions and other terms

   *He **wouldn't** share his blocks.*
   *She was **dreamin'** of love.*

- to create plurals with single numbers and letters

   *He just entered the terrible **2's**.*
   *You should capitalize all of the **T's**.*

APOSTROPHES + POSSESSION

It is common to see words that end in **s** not have the extra **'s**.

   *Johann Strauss**'s** music is beautiful.*
   CORRECT
   *Johann Strauss**'** music is beautiful.*
   CORRECT

In compound words, add an **'s** to the last word.

   *My brother-in-law**'s** house is beautiful.*

Do not use an apostrophe:

- with any of the possessive pronouns

   his, hers, its, ours, yours, theirs

- with numerical plurals that are not possessive

   the 1990s

APOSTROPHES + COMMON CONTRACTIONS

A word form called a **contraction** uses an apostrophe to shorten certain word phrases, as in *could not = couldn't*. Common contractions include:

- With forms of the verb TO BE

    I'm, we're, you're, he's, she's, it's, they're, where's,
    what's, when's, why's, how's

- With forms of the verb TO HAVE

    I've, we've, you've, they've, could've, would've, should've

- With the future expression WILL

    I'll, we'll, you'll, he'll, she'll, it'll, they'll

- With the verb DID

    why'd, where'd

- To express negation with NOT

    aren't, isn't, don't, doesn't, didn't, hasn't, haven't, wasn't, weren't,
    can't, couldn't, won't, wouldn't, shouldn't, mightn't, mustn't, needn't

- Others
    let's (let us), 'tis (it is), 'twas (it was)

QUOTATION MARKS

Quotation marks are used (in pairs):

- to enclose direct quotes

    George said, "Good night, Gracie."

- to identify titles of books, movies, and other published works

    Emma loved "The Lion King."

(**Note:** *It is standard practice in publishing to italicize published works.*)

- to identify technical, unusual terms, and nonstandard expressions

    During the pandemic, the college friends formed a "quaranteam."

CLOSING QUOTATION MARKS

Be sure to always include commas and periods inside closing quotation marks. Question marks and exclamation points are placed inside closing quotation marks when they are part of the quoted material; colons and semicolons are placed outside.

"I would like a cup of coffee," she told the waiter.

He replied, "I agree completely."

She asked her friend, "What did you say to the clerk?"

"Oh my!" he yelled.

Jeff asked for "time off"; his boss did not grant it.

SINGLE QUOTATION MARKS

Single quotation marks are used (in pairs):

- to enclose quotes inside a direct quote

The student wrote, "At summer camp, the motto was 'carpe diem'—'seize the day.'"

- to enclose a quote inside a headline

Mayoral Candidate Claims 'Victory'

COLON

A colon is used:

- to separate two independent clauses when the second clause illustrates or explains the first clause

The table was made out of walnut: walnut is one of the most durable hardwoods.

- to introduce an item or list of items following a sentence or an independent clause

The family had many pets: five cats, four dogs, three birds, and two fish.

- to introduce a list of bulleted items or numbered items

Follow these steps:
- *Get tissue.*
- *Blow nose.*
- *Throw tissue away.*

- to introduce a long quote or quotation

The preamble starts as follows:
We the People of the United States, in Order to form a more perfect Union, establish Justice, insure domestic Tranquility, provide for the common defense, promote the general Welfare, and secure the Blessings of Liberty to ourselves and our Posterity, do ordain and establish this Constitution for the United States of America.

- at the end of the greeting in formal correspondence

Dear Madam Speaker:

- in numerical expressions

  · Time expressions: *12:01*
  · Mathematical ratios: *4:1*
  · Certain references: *Luke 10:27*

- between a book's title and subtitle

Everyday Grammar Made Easy: A Quick Review of Everything You Forgot You Knew

A colon should *not* be used:

- between a preposition and a series of objects

The box was full of: toys, balls, and books.
(INCORRECT)

- after a phrase that is not an independent clause

She has several favorite colors, including: crimson red, forest green, and canary yellow.
(INCORRECT)

SEMICOLON

A semicolon introduces a pause that is slightly longer than a comma and is used:

- to join two independent clauses that are roughly balanced and related in thought

The house was quiet; all the children were asleep.

AVOID COMMA SPLICES

A **comma splice** is when a comma is used to separate two independent clauses. To fix a comma splice, use either (1) a semicolon or colon, (2) create two separate sentences from the independent clauses, or (3) add a coordinating conjunction (see page 84) and a comma.

The fall months are mild, October is no exception.
(INCORRECT)

(1) *The fall months are mild; October is no exception.*
(CORRECT)

(2) *The fall months are mild. October is no exception.*
(CORRECT)

(3) *The fall months are mild, and October is no exception.*
(CORRECT)

- before a conjunctive adverb (see page 81) that connects two independent clauses.

    *They meant to clean the house; **however**, they ran out of time.*

- before a coordinating conjunction (see page 84) that joins independent clauses when at least one of the clauses contains commas

    *The kids went to the special Disney theater; **and** they saw "Pinocchio," "Bambi," and "Frozen."*

- to separate a series of phrases or clauses when they contain commas

    They planned to visit ballparks in Houston, Texas; Atlanta, Georgia; and Philadelphia, Pennsylvania.

A semicolon should not be used:

- when a dependent clause precedes an independent clause

While it snowed; the hikers took shelter.
(INCORRECT)

HYPHEN

A hyphen is used:

- to connect a compound (two-word) adjective when it occurs before the noun modified

*He was exhausted from his **five-mile** run.*

- in prefixes involving proper nouns

*See you in **mid**-October!*

- with a variety of prefixes, usually to show clarity

***semi**-soft cheese, **mini**-series*

Note: Nowadays, it's common to not use hyphens with some prefixes

***semi**soft cheese, **mini**series*

- to indicate the age of someone when used as an adjective

***four-year-old** boy*

- with certain family relationships

great-uncle, great-great-grandmother

- to indicate a fraction when written in words (not numbers)

one–fourth, three–sixteenths

- to connect the parts of all numbers from 21 to 99 when written in words

twenty–three, fifty–seven

- to mark a break between syllables and compound words that occur at the end of a line of text

They went fly–
fishing but did not catch a thing.

(Note: Hyphens should not be used as dashes. Also, spaces should not be inserted to precede or follow a hyphen.)

EN DASH AND EM DASH

The **en dash** is longer than a hyphen because it is set to equal the width of the letter *N*. The **em dash** is longer than an en dash and is it set to equal the width of the letter *M*.

An **en dash** is used:
- to indicate a number range

Read pages 3–13, then write a short summary.
She usually runs 5–7 miles.

- to connect already hyphenated terms

low-sugar–high-fiber foods

An **em dash** is used:

- to replace commas in an offset word, phrase, or clause to improve readability

They wanted to buy the house, but—just minutes before they got their offer in—a competing offer was made.

- in place of parentheses to create more informality

He sold his truck—his one true love—because he needed cash badly.

- in place of a colon to bring emphasis

The student finally heard from the University—admitted!

- to add an aside or to add a contrast

He was very tired—even though he slept all day—and decided to go to the party.

- to indicate omitted content (usually with two or three em dashes in succession)

She used words in her rant against the authorities, including ——.

PARENTHESES ( )

Parentheses are used (in pairs):

- to enclose information intended as an aside, which is related to but not essential to the main idea being expressed

The couple bought a new Aspen (a VW).

- to indicate an optional ending

book(s)

- to group factors in numerical expressions

$$6 \times (11 - 4) = 42$$

A PERIOD BEFORE OR AFTER PARENTHESES?

If the enclosed expression occurs at the end of a sentence, the period goes outside the parenthesis. If the parenthetical information is a complete sentence, the terminal period should be placed inside the parenthesis.

The professor did not agree (even though it was a good idea).

The professor did not agree. (Even though she thought is was a good idea.)

BRACKETS [ ]

Brackets are used (in pairs):

* to insert supplementary information without changing the meaning of the surrounding text

    Chris moved to the next topic [Slide 6].

* in a quotation to show divergence from spelling or punctuation used in the source material

    She said, "[T]his heritage was reflected in its form."

ELLIPSIS (. . .)

An ellipsis is used:

* to indicate omitted word(s) from a quoted passage

    "I pledge allegiance . . . to the United States of America."

* to suggest hesitation or a shift in expression

    I'd like to go . . . No, I better not.

* at the end of a sentence to indicate a complete thought that trails off

    The living conditions left a lot to be desired . . .

SLASH (/)

A slash is used:

- to show connected concepts

  town/gown, den/study, work/life

- to stand in for the word *or* with alternatives

  yes/no, his/her, if/when

- to stand in for the word *per* in ratios

  miles/hour, P/E, teaspoons/gallon

- to facilitate certain informal abbreviations (without the use of periods)

  w/o (without), c/o (care of), m/s (manuscript)

- to serve as a delimiter or an operator with certain numbers

  fractions (3/4), dates (01/01/21, 1998/9)

- to show poetic line breaks when written in prose

  Jack and Jill / went up a hill / to fetch a pail of water.

*(**Note:** In spelling, a space is used before and after the slash only in the last circumstance—when used to indicate line breaks. In general, spaces should not be inserted, unless needed to enhance readability.)*

FORWARD (/) AND BACKWARD (\) SLASHES

The traditional slash used as a character is referred to as a **forward slash** (/) in technical coding and writing (and web addresses—*http://*). **The backward slash (\)** is also periodically used in such contexts; however, the back slash is not generally used as a punctuation mark.

– FORMATTING TOOLS –

In addition to use of punctuation marks, the other way that we can affect meaning with visual tools is by manipulating the appearance of letters and words themselves through the use of capital letters and altering the "face" of the fonts used with *italics*, **bolding**, and <u>underlining</u>.

CAPITALIZATION

The rules for capitalizing the initial letters of words are straightforward. Use initial capitals:

* with the first word of every sentence, which is called **sentence case**

  In the beginning was the Word.

* with the first word of a quoted sentence

  Piglet asked, "How do you spell love?"

* with all personal names

  Michael Jordan, Dave

* with all proper nouns

  Tuesday, Thanksgiving, Chicago Bears

- with the first-person, singular pronoun *I*

  I think, therefore I am.

- when the first-person, singular pronoun *I* is used in a contraction form

  I'm, I'll

- with a person's title when used before a name

  Dr. Seuss

- In direct address

  Greetings, Doctor.

- with the first word of titles of publications and creative works—except for articles, prepositions, and conjunctions—which is called **headline** (aka **title**) **case**

  The World According to Garp

Note: There is a current trend in formatting publication titles to move away from headline case and toward sentence case, which only capitalizes the first word of the title and proper nouns.

  The Cat in the Hat → *The cat in the hat*
  (HEADLINE CASE)   (SENTENCE CASE)

- with acronyms (usually without periods)

  NATO, UNICEF

Do not capitalize:

- the four seasons

  spring, summer, fall winter

- the first word of a list after a colon in the middle of a sentence

They had emergency supplies: flares, water, a candle, matches, and ponchos.

ALL CAPS

You should generally avoid using ALL CAPITAL letters in your writing, unless you do so intentionally. ALL CAPS often convey a sense of shouting and can be taken as rude or offensive. Be especially sensitive to this in texts, emails, and other electronic messaging, where there is often not much context around the communication. When communicating electronically or in printed media, there are a number of ways that the actual appearance of the type can be modified to affect interpretation and meaning.

Italicized type is used:

- with titles (in lieu of quotation marks)

  The Giving Tree

- with foreign words and phrases

  laissez faire, Bon apétit!

- to identify a word as a word

  The writer's favorite word is *word.*

- with words meant to mimic sounds

  The cow goes *mooooo*, and the bee goes *buzzzz.*

Bolded type is used:

- as one option used in distinguishing document titles, subtitles, and headers

  Chapter 1, Section 3, Appendix.

- to highlight words visually

  *"There is a **reason** for it all."*

<u>**Underlined type**</u> (also called **underscored type**) works essentially the same as bolded type to highlight words

<u>Editor's Note</u>
You need to sign all <u>five</u> pages.

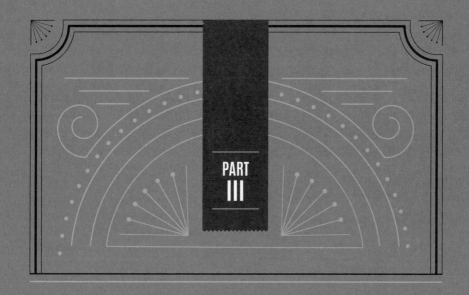

PART
III

COMMON
PITFALLS

CHAPTER 10

MISUSE OF SAME-SOUNDING WORDS

One of the challenges with grammar is that if you are not familiar with or confident of underlying grammar details, it is difficult to recognize your own errors and opportunities for improvement. In this chapter, you will find numerous examples of common mistakes that people make regularly and frequently, focusing specifically on errors resulting from the confusion of same-sound or similar-sounding words, such as *their* and *there*. In each example, the incorrect usage is on the left and in *red* and the correct usage is on the right and in **bold** type. Pay special attention to those items where the example in red seems correct to you.

HOMOPHONES + HOMOGRAPHS

Homophones are words that sound the same but have different meanings—*fare* and *fair*.
Homographs are words that have the same spelling but have different meanings—*lead* (*not follow*) and *lead* (*in the pencil*). Combining both of these groups, **homonyms** are words that either sound or are spelled the same but have different meanings such as the noun *bat* versus the verb *bat*.

ACCEPT | EXCEPT

She agreed to except the job offer. | *She agreed to **accept** the job offer.*

Accept is a verb that means to take or to receive, so that is the correct verb in this example. *Except* is generally used as a preposition or conjunction. When used as a verb, except means to exclude.

*The gym teacher **excepted** the student from the day's workout requirements.*

ADVICE | ADVISE

The teacher gave good advise. | *The teacher gave good **advice**.*

Advice is a noun; *advise* is a verb.

*People who **advise** sometimes give good **advice**.*

AFFECT | EFFECT

She had a positive affect on the kids. | *She had a positive **effect** on the kids.*

Effect is usually a noun, which is called for in this example. When used as a verb, effect means to accomplish or to make happen. *Affect*, on the other hand, is usually a verb that means to change or to influence.

*The ruling **affected** the outcome.*

*If you want to have a positive **effect**, you need to **affect** things in a positive way!*
                          NOUN   VERB

Note: *When used as a noun, often in psychology, affect suggests feeling or emotion.*

ALLUSION | ILLUSION

The magician's trick was an optical allusion.	*The magician's trick was an optical **illusion**.*

These are both nouns, but use of *allusion* is pretty rare, as it means a casual or reference to something.

*The poet used the word "trick" as an **allusion** to magic.*

ALOT | A LOT | ALLOT

They made alot of money that summer.	*They made **a lot** of money that summer.*

Alot is a common misspelling. The phrase *a lot*, used to refer to many or to a great extent, should be spelled in two words. There is also the verb *allot* (meaning to apportion), which occasionally is misused for *a lot*.

ALREADY | ALL READY

The team was already to depart. | *The team was **all ready** to depart.*

All ready is a phrase used as an adjective to mean prepared. *Already*, as one word, serves as an adverb that is used to describe something that happened previously.

*I had **already** departed by the time the team left.*

ALTAR | ALTER

Nothing will altar my plans. | *Nothing will **alter** my plans.*

Alter is a verb signifying to bring change, while *altar* is a noun that refers to a special place in which religious rites are performed.

*The bride and groom met at the **altar**.*

AS SOON | ASSUME

I would just assume leave the party. | *I would just as soon leave the party.*

Just as soon itself is a little cryptic, but it is suggesting that I would sooner leave the party or prefer to leave the party. Use of *assume*—a verb that is not meaningful in this placement—no doubt results from someone mishearing the phrase *as soon.*

I assume you want to leave the party.

CAPITAL | CAPITOL

White House should begin with capitol letters. | *White House should begin with capital letters.*

The word *capitol*, ending in *-ol*, has a very narrow meaning that refers to a building used for legislative purposes either at the state or federal level.

The state legislature meets in the capitol.

COMPLEMENT | COMPLIMENT

He gave the sculptor a wonderful complement. | *He gave the sculptor a wonderful compliment.*

The word *complement* refers to a part that makes something complete. A *compliment* is a word of praise or admiration.

The wine was a perfect complement to the beef fondue.

COMPLEMENTARY | COMPLIMENTARY

The price of admission was complementary. | *The price of admission was complimentary.*

Complimentary can mean free. It can also mean praising, as in:

The teacher was very complimentary of the student's performance.

In contrast, *complementary* suggests a good fit, as in:

Their work styles were complementary.

CONFIDENT | CONFIDANT

The coach was confidant in her players. | *The coach was **confident** in her players.*

This sentence calls for an adjective, and *confident* is an adjective that means having assurance. *Confidant*, on the other hand, is a noun identifying a person in whom others can confide.

*The coach served as a **confidant** to the injured player.*

CONSCIOUS | CONSCIENCE

She has a guilty conscious from not studying enough. | *She has a guilty **conscience** from not studying enough.*

One's *conscience*, a noun, is characterized as an inner voice or feeling that serves as a moral guide. In contrast, *conscious* is an adjective that affirms an awake or alert state.

*The patient is now **conscious** of her surroundings.*

DESERT | DESSERT

I want to skip dinner and go straight to desert. | *I want to skip dinner and go straight to **dessert**.*

These are both nouns. *Desert* (with one S) is a vast, sandy expanse. *Dessert* is a tasty end-of-meal treat.

*After **dessert**, let's take a **desert** ride in the four-wheeler.*

EVERYDAY | EVERY DAY

I speak correctly everyday. | *I speak correctly **every day**.*

When the words of the adverb phrase *every day* are combined in one, it becomes an adjective (*everyday*).

*I try to be accurate in my **everyday** speaking.*

INTO | IN TO

*They moved **in to** a new place.* | *They moved **into** a new place.*

The preposition *into* should be spelled as one word. *In* and *to* as separate words are not meaningful in a phrase. Spelling *into* in two words (*in to*) is a misspelling.

ITS | IT'S

Its my belief. | ***It's** my belief.*

It's is a contraction—a shortened form of *it + is*—and is the correct form for this sentence. *Its* is the possessive form of the inanimate pronoun *it*.

*The bird tweeted **its** tune.*

ITS/IT'S AND LETS/LET'S

Errors made in using these terms are fairly common and noticeable, so it is worthwhile to look at these. The key to both is to recognize and remember that *it's* is a contraction of it + is and *let's* is a contraction of let + us.

LETS | LET'S

Lets get out of here. | ***Let's** get out of here.*

Let's is a contraction—a shortened form of *let* and *us*—and is the correct form for this sentence. *Lets* is simply the third-person singular form of the verb TO LET.

*The babysitter **lets** the child sleep late on Fridays.*

LOSE | LOOSE

The toddler's shoes were too lose, and he tripped. | *The toddler's shoes were too **loose**, and he tripped.*

Though appearing similar, these words do not share any common meaning. *Loose* is an adjective describing something that is not tight fitting (like toddler's shoes). *Lose* is a verb used in the context of misplacing something or not winning something.

*I'm all in. If I **lose**, I will **lose** it all.*

MORAL | MORALE

Weak leadership led to low moral among the troops. | *Weak leadership led to low **morale** among the troops.*

Morale is a noun referring to attitudes within a person or group, while the word *moral* is an adjective meaning ethical.

*The teen was faced with a **moral** dilemma.*

PEEK | PEAK | PIQUE

The peek of the mountain seemed so far away. | *The **peak** of the mountain seemed so far away.*

Peak is a noun representing the high point or pinnacle of something—a mountain, contagion, human performance, and the like. *Peek* is a verb that describes a quick look. The word *pique*, with the same sound as peek and peak, refers to a feeling of irritation.

*The new dad **peeked** in the nursery to see if the baby was still asleep.*

PERSONAL | PERSONNEL

Her experience was too personnel to share with others. | *Her experience was too **personal** to share with others.*

Personnel—a collective noun referring to the people who work in an organization—is confused in this example with *personal*—an adjective describing something private to an individual.

*The office **personnel** were out in force.*

PRINCIPAL | PRINCIPLE

Holding firm on this | *Holding firm on this*
is a matter of principal. | *is a matter of **principle**.*

Principle is correct in this context, as it is a noun and refers to a legal or an ethical standard. *Principal*, in contrast, can be an adjective that means *main* and a noun that names a position of high authority.

*The **principal** argument was not found to be persuasive.*

PROPHECY | PROPHESY

The recluse came to prophecy an | *The recluse came to **prophesy** an*
imminent end of the world. | *imminent end of the world.*

Prophesy is a verb—to predict or to foretell and is the correct word in this example. *Prophecy* is a noun that means the prediction or foretelling that comes from the prophesying.

*The **prophecy** for the future was gloomy.*

THEIR | THERE | THEY'RE

They all have there own views. | *They all have **their** own views.*

Their is a possessive pronoun adjective and is the correct word for this usage. *There* is an adverb meaning "in a place." *They're* is a contraction of *they + are*, and *they* is a third-person plural subject pronoun. If you have some uncertainty in using these terms, it might help to spend more time studying pronoun use.

***Their** favorite movie is on TV tonight.*
POSSESSIVE PRONOUN ADJECTIVE
*The line for the movie is over **there**.*
ADVERB
***They're** waiting in the lobby.*
CONTRACTION OF THEY + ARE

THEN | THAN

We are better then this. | *We are better **than** this.*

The word *than*, a conjunction, is used in comparisons.

*Olaf is a better ball player **than** Al.*

The word *then*, an adverb, is used in time sequence statements.

*Al started to play first, **then** Olaf followed a year later.*

TO | TOO | TWO

I love you to much for my own good. | *I love you **too** much for my own good.*

The word *too*, with two Os, is an adverb that can mean *also*, *very*, and *to an excessive degree* (as in the example above). The word *two*, including a W, is a number. If usage calls for a preposition and not an adverb or a number, the word *to* should be used.

*Take it **to** the bank.*
PREPOSITION
*I love you, **too**.*
ADVERB
*I would like **two** bagels.*
NUMBER

WHO'S | WHOSE

Who's book is that? | ***Whose** book is that?*

This question is about ownership (or belongingness), asking in effect—To whom does this book belong?—so it calls for the possessive form *whose*. *Who's* is a contraction of *who* + *is*.

***Who's** coming to dinner?*

WHO'S/WHOSE

Like we saw with *it's* and *let's* in this chapter, it is helpful here to recognize that **who's** is a contraction of *who + is*. The possessive form of who is **whose** and is the right word to use to denote possession, as in *Whose car is that?*

YOUR | YOU'RE

Your never going to believe it. | *You're never going to believe it.*

You're is a contraction—a shortened form of *you + are*—and is the correct form for this sentence. *Your* is the possessive form of the pronoun *you*.

Your accomplishments are so impressive.

CHAPTER 11
MISAPPLICATION OF GRAMMAR PRINCIPLES

As noted in chapter 10, one of the challenges with grammar is that it can be difficult to recognize your own errors and opportunities for improvement. In this chapter, you will find numerous examples of mistakes that people make regularly and frequently, focusing specifically on errors directly related to usage issues, such as the misuse of *between* or *among*. In each example, the incorrect usage is on the left and in *red* and the correct usage is on the right and in **bold** type. Pay special attention to those items where the example in red seems correct to you.

AIN'T | ISN'T

There ain't no way. | *There **isn't** any way.*

Ain't is a term that is used colloquially to express *am not, is not, are not, has not,* and *have not,* but it is considered a nonstandard contraction and a word that should only be used in informal settings.

AND or BUT (TO BEGIN A SENTENCE)

The question posed in this example: *Is it okay to start a sentence with a conjunction?* The "rule of thumb" advice historically has been *no*—to avoid starting a sentence in this way. However, common practice today is to support such use as a natural way to communicate. The use is still generally discouraged in more formal writing.

***But** she will never understand. **And** that made me extremely angry.*

AT or WITH or FOR (TO END A SENTENCE)

The question posed in this example: *Is it okay to end a sentence with a preposition?* The "rule of thumb" advice historically has been *no*—to avoid ending a sentence in this way. However, common practice today is to support such use as a natural way to communicate. The use is still generally discouraged in more formal writing.

*Whom are you going out **with**?*

BETWEEN | AMONG

The kids had a choice between three different flavors. | *The kids had a choice among three different flavors.*

Both of these prepositions are used to refer to a selection within a set of multiple items. A common misconception is that you use *between* if there are two items in the set and *among* if there are three or more items in the set, but the actual convention is more involved. *Between* is the word of choice when distinctly naming two or more individual items.

*Discussions **between** the superintendent, the school board, and the PTA officers are continuing.*

Among is the word of choice when referring to a group of three or more unnamed elements.

*Discussions **among** all key school constituencies are continuing.*

BRING | TAKE

Don't forget to bring your lunchbox to school. | *Don't forget to take your lunchbox to school.*

These two verbs involve moving something from one place to another. Use *bring* when the movement is toward your location (as speaker).

*Can you **bring me** the camera?*

Use *take* when the movement is away from your location (as speaker) to a different place.

*Can you **take** the camera in for repair?*

CAN | MAY

Can I use your bathroom? | *May I use your bathroom?*

May is a word that is used to ask for permission, so it is the better word to use in this context. *Can* is asking *is it possible?* On the other hand, *can* is used very frequently in permission-asking situations, and it is considered acceptable in informal conversation.

Can I lift that barbell?

COMMA SPLICES

The day was beautiful, | *The day was beautiful.*
the sun was shining. | *The sun was shining.*

A **comma splice** occurs when two independent clauses are connected by a comma, which is incorrect. This can come across as a careless error in punctuation. Instead of using a comma, the thoughts can be expressed in independent sentences, as above.

Alternatively, a colon could be used since the second clause is an illustration of the first.

The day was beautiful: the sun was shining.

Or a semicolon could be used since the independent clauses are balanced in construction.

The day was beautiful; the sun was shining.

Or a comma and coordinating conjunction can be added.

*The day was beautiful, **and** the sun was shining.*

DANGLING MODIFIERS

Breaking through the pasture fence, the man had to fix the slats.	*Breaking through the pasture fence,* **the horse** *caused the man to have to fix the slats.*

A modifier is a word, phrase, or clause that serves to add information to another word in order to enhance the overall meaning, and it should always be clear which word is being modified. If there is a modifier in place without the target word present in the sentence, that results in a dangling modifier and should be avoided.

DO'S AND DON'TS

How should I spell "dos and don'ts" in a sentence?	*How should I spell* **"do's and don'ts"** *in a sentence?*

Typically, an apostrophe is not involved in making a singular noun plural, but sometimes an apostrophe is introduced to minimize confusion, such as with single letters—*A's and B's*. In the example cited above, *do* should probably get an apostrophe (*do's*) because *dos* may be confusing. But *don't* already has an apostrophe, and adding another one—*don't's*—to be consistent with *do's* would be awkward. Given the exception that this situation represents, the *Chicago Manual of Style* recommends *dos and don'ts*, and the *Associated Press* recommends *do's and don'ts*.

DOUBLE NEGATIVES

You don't have to do nothing before the guests arrive.	*You* **don't** *have to* **do** **anything** *before the guests arrive.*

The problem occurs when two negative words are used in the same sentence. In effect, the two negatives cancel each other out and create a positive statement, but often the result is confusing. In general, use of double negatives is discouraged.

EACH | EVERY | ALL

The words *each* and *every* both refer to a singular item or person. The key difference is that *each* refers to an individual item or person.

*I would like to taste **each** flavor.*

Every refers to a group of items or people treated as one.

*I would like to taste **every** flavor.*

The word *all* is used with plural nouns.

*I would like to taste **all** flavors.*

EITHER | NEITHER | BOTH

These words come into play when you are dealing with two items or choices. *Either* is used in selections of one *or* the other—**either** *this or that.* *Both* is used in selections of one *and* the other—**both** *this and that. Neither* is used in rejections of both—**neither** *this nor that.* In terms of subject/verb agreement:

If both of the choices are singular, the verb should be singular.

*Either the dog or the cat **has** fleas.*

If one or both of the choices are plural, the verb should be plural.

*Neither the dog nor the cats **have** fleas.*

FARTHER | FURTHER

| *He needs to think farther about the offer.* | *He needs to think **further** about the offer.* |

Both of these words relate to the concept of more distant. The key distinction is that *farther* refers exclusively to physical distance, while *further* refers to more figurative distance, as in the example above.

*The boy hit the ball **farther** than he ever had before.*

FEWER | LESS

I got less Snickers | *I got **fewer** Snickers*
for Halloween this year. | *for Halloween this year.*

If the noun that you are describing is countable, then use *fewer*.

*There are **fewer** boats in the regatta this spring.*

If the noun that you are describing is general and not countable, then use *less*.

*I would like **less** milk in my cereal, please.*

GOOD | WELL

The job was done good. | *The job was done **well**.*

Even though these words are often used in place of each other, they have distinct usage rules. *Good* is an adjective. Thus, it modifies a noun to make something good—*a good meal, a good day's work*. Meanwhile, *well* is an adverb. Thus, it modifies a verb to indicate something done well—*the assignment was completed well, the meal was well prepared*. There is a bit of an overlap between the two words when considering *well* in the context of health. *Good wishes* and *well wishes* are both acceptable when expressing hope for someone's recovery.

GOOD VERSUS WELL

The key to correct usage of these two frequently used words is to remember that **good** is an adjective that modifies nouns and **well** is an adverb that modifies verbs. So, if you want to tell someone that your day was favorable, you would think, *day* is a noun, so I need to use the adjective good: *I had a good day*. On the other hand, if you want to tell someone that how things went were favorable, you would think, *went* is a verb, so I need to use the adverb well: *Things went well*.

HANGED | HUNG

I hanged the picture on the wall | *I **hung** the picture on the wall.*

Hung is the past tense form of the verb TO HANG when the hanging is anything other than the suspension of a person by a rope.

*The Old West outlaw was **hanged** in the noonday sun.*

HYPHEN | DASH | EN DASH | EM DASH

The *hyphen* (-) is a punctuation mark that is used to join words (*twenty-one*) or parts of words (like a hyphen break in a word at the end of a line). The dash comes in two lengths that are both longer than a hyphen. An *en dash* (–) is the width of the letter N. The *em dash* (—) is the width of the letter M.

While they are often used interchangeably, the *en dash* is most often used to indicate a range instead of a hyphen.

The temperature will reach 75–80 degrees by afternoon.

The *em dash* is most often used to indicate a pause in the sentence.

The climber reached a precipice—now what?

I.E. | E.G.

These are two Latin abbreviations that are used in writing frequently, and often they are used incorrectly. Many writers use them interchangeably, thinking they mean the same thing. In Latin, *i.e.* stands for *id est*, which means *that is*. So, you would use *i.e.* to suggest *namely* or *in other words*.

*He was ready to go, **i.e.**, he missed his family.*

In contrast, *e.g.* stands for *exempli gratia*, which means *for example*.

*He had many good times, **e.g.**, his 30th birthday party at the beach.*

Note: *These abbreviations are often italicized and usually offset by commas.*

IF I WAS | IF I WERE

If I was rich, I'd buy a big house. | *If I **were** rich, I'd buy a big house.*

The use of *was* in an "if" statement is correct if it is something that could have actually happened now or in the past (indicative mood). The use of *were* in an "if" statement is correct if it is something that is hypothetical or desirable.

INFER | IMPLY

*In her remarks, she **inferred*** | *In her remarks, she **implied***
that I needed to leave. | *that I needed to leave.*

A speaker *implies*; a listener *infers*.

*He can **infer** from her inaction that she's not interested.*

INSURE | ENSURE

*The mom wants to **insure** that her* | *The mom wants to **ensure** that her*
daughter makes the team. | *daughter makes the team.*

Ensure means to make sure that something happens, as this sentence suggests. *Insure*, on the other hand, is to get protective coverage for something.

*The mom will **insure** her daughter now that she has passed her driving test.*

IT IS I, IT WAS I | IT IS ME, IT WAS ME

Traditionally, the grammar rules suggest that *It is I* or *It was I* is the correct way to express this type of thought. *Is*, as a form of the verb TO BE, would typically call for a subject pronoun (see page 38). Because it sounds somewhat stilted, however, both forms are accepted—one as a more formal way (*It is I, It is she*), the other as a more casual way (*it's me, it is her*).

LAY | LIE

I need to lay down. | *I need to **lie** down.*

As verbs, TO LAY is transitive and requires a direct object, while TO LIE is intransitive and does not. So, you can *lay* a carpet, but you *lie* on deck chair.

LYING VERSUS LAYING

While we know that one *lies* on a bed and that a hen *lays* eggs, it's common to become confused when these verbs change forms. The past tense of TO LIE is *lay*:

*"Today I **lie** down. Yesterday I **lay** down."*

Below are participles for both verbs.

	PRESENT	PAST	PRESENT PARTICIPLE	PAST PARTICIPLE
TO LIE	lie	lay	lying	lain

	PRESENT	PAST	PRESENT PARTICIPLE	PAST PARTICIPLE
TO LAY	lay	laid	laying	laid

ME | I (ALONG WITH OTHERS)

Me and her are planning to go. | ***She and I** are planning to go.*

Him and me are planning to go. | ***He and I** are planning to go.*

When pronouns are used as a subject, subject pronouns should be used. When pronouns are used as objects, object pronouns should be used (see pages 38–39 for the various pronoun forms).

MISPLACED MODIFIERS

The man drove the silver car wearing his hat.	*The man, **wearing his hat**, drove the silver car.*

Generally, with adjective modifiers, single-word adjectives should immediately precede the noun (*the **silver** car*), and an adjective phrase should immediately follow the noun (*the car, **painted in silver** . . .*). If a modifier is not close to the noun, a reader may be confused regarding the intended meaning. For example, in the incorrect example above, is the car wearing the man's hat?

NOT I | NOT ME

Similar to the *It is I* entry earlier, traditional grammar would establish "not I" as a correct negative response to the question, *Who did it?* The phrase "not I" is a shortcut to "It was not I." But "*not me*" is so common that it is considered an acceptable informal response.

NUMBER | AMOUNT

*The piggy bank has a large **amount** of pennies.*	*The piggy bank has a large **number** of pennies.*

Both *number* and *amount* refer to a quantity of something, and the nature of the something determines which term to use. If the noun associated with the terms is a **countable noun**—pencils, plums, pennies—then the term *number* would be appropriate. If the noun associated with the term is an **uncountable noun**—fear, food, freedom—then the term *amount* would be appropriate.

A NUMBER | THE NUMBER

A number of missing soldiers is a concern.	***The number** of missing soldiers is a concern.*

The subject *A number* takes a plural verb. The subject *The number* takes a singular verb, as in this example.

*A number of cupcakes **are** in need of more icing.*

OF | HAVE

*I would **of** come earlier if I had known.* | *I would **have** come earlier if I had known.*

The past tense of these modal verbs are *could have*, *should have*, and *would have* and are combined with a past participle.

> *could have*—refers to something possible for you to do that you did not do
> *should have*—refers to something good for you to do that you did not do
> *would have*—refers to something you wanted to do but did not do

When the contracted forms of these verb phrases—could've, should've, would've—are spoken, they sound like *could of, should of, would of*. This explains why some people incorrectly use *of* instead of *have* in writing.

PREPOSITION (TO END A SENTENCE)

*See entry **AT or WITH or FOR***

REAL | REALLY

*She was **real** happy with her new job.* | *She was **really** happy with her new job.*

The word *real* is an adjective that means genuine, authentic, not imagined. The word *really* is an adverb that means actually, very, thoroughly. They are not interchangeable, but people do accept real in place of really in informal American English conversation.

REGARDLESS | IRREGARDLESS

*I went to the party **irregardless** of my physical condition.* | *I went to the party **regardless** of my physical condition.*

Irregardless is considered a "nonstandard" spelling of *regardless*, which means that it is *not* a word recognized by many grammarians. Since irregardless is intended to mean the same thing as regardless—"without regard to"—you would do well to stick with regardless.

RUN-ON SENTENCES

The dog ate my homework there wasn't time to do it over.	*The dog ate my homework, and there wasn't time to do it over.* **OR** *The dog ate my homework. There wasn't time to do it over.*

Run-on sentences occur when two (or more) independent clauses are attached but are incorrectly connected or punctuated. To correct a run-on sentence, a **coordinating conjunction** (see page 84) can be added, as above, or the clauses can be detached and presented as separate sentences.

SENTENCE FRAGMENTS

The problems were bad. Such as people not wearing masks and not maintaining social distance.	*The problems were bad from people not wearing masks and not maintaining social distance.*

A sentence fragment is an incomplete sentence. It can be identified with the complete thought test—*Does the sentence have a subject and predicate, and is it sensible on its own?* Some fragments result from a missing subject, others result from a missing verb, and others have superfluous words present.

SET | SIT

Come set for a while and rest your feet. | *Come **sit** for a while and rest your feet.*

Set is a transitive verb that requires an object. In other words, when you use the verb TO SET, you need to set something, such as *set a* goal or *set a* date or *set an item down*. In the example above, you could *set a coffee down*, but you cannot *set*. You *sit,* because sit is an intransitive verb and does not require an object.

THAN I | THAN ME (IN COMPARISON)

You have a much nicer car than me. | *You have a much nicer car than **I**.*

If you complete the thought in your mind, you realize that a word is assumed and not stated—the word *do*.

*You have a much nicer care than I **do**.*

With this, the correct version is more evident. Like other grammar situations, however, people commonly use *me* in constructions like this, and such usage is accepted in informal communication.

THIS/THESE | THAT/THOSE

This and *these* are pronouns and adjectives that identify things that are close to the speaker in space or time.

This *new mystery is one of the best I have read.*

That and *those* are pronouns and adjectives that identify things that are more distant from the speaker in space or time.

Those *mountains are beautiful in the sunset.*

USE TO | USED TO

*I **use to** live in that town.* | *I **used to** live in that town.*

The past tense form of TO USE, *used*, is appropriate in describing something that happened in the past, as in this example. Similarly, it can help describe something that is familiar.

*He is **used to** this situation.*

So, generally, the past tense phrase, *used to*, is most common, although *use to* can be linked with *did* to create the same sense.

*It **didn't use** to work this way.*
***Did** you **use to** have this job?*

WHO | THAT | WHICH

These words are pronouns that introduce clauses.

Who always refers to people—to a person or a group of people.

> *Many of the seniors **who** graduated will go to accomplish big things.*

That and *which* are used to refer to things and groups (although *that* is sometimes used with people).

> *Those glasses, **which** are all broken, need to be replaced.*

That introduces an **essential clause**—one that is necessary to the meaning of the sentence and is *not* set off by commas.

> *The house **that** sits on the corner is on fire.*

Which introduces a **nonessential clause**—one that adds supplemental information to the sentence in a clause that is often set off by commas.

> *The house, **which** was built in 1985, is on fire.*

The inappropriate use of *that* and *which* will not particularly stand out in your speaking or writing, but using them correctly will attest to attentive grammar use.

WHEN TO USE *THAT* AND *WHICH*?

One of the most frequent challenges that people encounter with *that* and *which* is determining the right one to use in a dependent clause describing the subject of a sentence. Let's use a movie as an example. Should I say, "The movie *that* I liked" or "The movie *which* I liked"? It depends on whether the clause is **essential** or **nonessential**. If it's essential, use *that*. If it's nonessential, use *which*.

> *The movie, **which** I liked, had great special effects.*
> (NONESSENTIAL, NEEDS COMMAS)

> *The movie **that** I liked had more special effects than a movie I did not like.*
> (ESSENTIAL, NO COMMAS)

WHO | WHOM

Who do you believe? | ***Whom** do you believe?*

If you convert this question to a statement, it becomes: *You do believe who/whom*, and this makes it clear that the pronoun is a direct object. The objective case (whom) is used for direct objects, indirect objects, and objects of the preposition. The subjective case (who) is used for subjects and predicate nominatives.

***Who** is the believer?*
PREDICATE NOMINATIVE = SUBJECT CASE

*Give it to Jack, for **whom** it was meant.*
OBJECT OF THE PREPOSITION = OBJECT CASE

WILL | SHALL

I shall go to the store later today. | *I **will** go to the store later today.*

It used to be expected that *shall* be used as the first person (*I, we*) form of the verb TO BE. This is not common in American English anymore, and *will* is typically preferred for all persons. *Shall* is still preferred with an offer or suggestion in the first person.

***Shall** I take your plate?*
***Shall** we go to the dance?*

Shall is also used in the second and third person to provide a sense of emphasis or command.

*You **shall** go to school.*
*She **shall** do her homework.*

– APPENDIX A: –
GLOSSARY OF GRAMMAR TERMS

This glossary compiles brief definitions of 150+ terms that are important to understanding the various facets of grammar. Most of these are also covered in more detail elsewhere in the previous chapters. Where appropriate, examples are provided to illustrate use of the terms. Use this glossary to refresh your understanding of significant grammar concepts and terms.

Active Voice: A construction in which the subject is the performer of the action expressed by the verb.

*The **cat watched** the bird in the garden.*

Adjective: A word used to modify a noun for description or clarification. There are two basic types of adjectives: *descriptive* and *limiting*.

*I saw a **spotted** frog.*

Adjective Phrase: A combination of words making up a phrase that as a whole serves as an adjective.

*The car, **ten years old today**, still runs smoothly.*

Adjective Series: A string of two or more adjectives, working together to modify a noun.

*The **old, abandoned, broken-down** vehicle needs to be removed.*

Adverb: A word used to modify a verb, an adjective, or another adverb. An adverb is invariable—it has neither gender nor number. It can indicate time, place, quality, intensity, and manner, and it generally answers the question *When?*, *Where?*, or *How?*

*She sang **softly** to her infant.*

Adverb Series: A string of two or more adverbs, working together to modify a verb, an adjective, or another adverb.

*She walked **quickly and quietly**.*

Affirmative Sentence: A sentence that states a fact or situation that is true, without negation.

He rides the jet ski expertly.

Affix: A word or part of a word added to another to augment its meaning. *See Prefix and Suffix.*

Agreement: A condition whereby different words in the same sentence must correspond in form to agree in gender, number, and/or person. In English, the most common forms of agreement are between subject and verb and between pronoun and antecedent. *See also Gender.*

Jack and Jill are siblings.

The wild horses are beautiful, and they love to roam.

Agreement (Pronoun and Noun): A condition calling for the agreement of a pronoun and its antecedent in gender, number, and person. *See also Gender.*

The man arrived at work, and he saw his client waiting.

Agreement (Subject and Verb): A condition calling for the agreement of a subject and its verb in number.

The stormy weather is frightening.

Antecedent: The noun or noun phrase referred to by a pronoun.

The little girl is sleeping. She needs to get up soon.

Articles: *a*, *an*, or *the* that precedes a noun to indicate its state of definiteness, whether it refers to a general person or thing (*a or an*) or to a particular person or thing (*the*).

I played with the puppy.

Augmentative: A word or an affix that is used to indicate a large size.

The opera house has a grand entrance.

Auxiliary Verb: *See Helping Verb.*

Case: *See Pronoun Case.*

Clause: A group of words that includes at least a subject and a verb and forms a sentence or part of a sentence.

*The museum, **which is well known**, burned in the fire.*

Collective Noun: A singular noun that signifies a group of persons or things.

*The **crowd** surrounds the stage.*

Common Noun: A noun signifying a thing in general.

*The **apple** looked delicious.*

Comparative: A form using adjectives or adverbs in the comparison of two things.

*Your phone is **newer** than mine.*

Comparative Adjective: An adjective involved in a comparative.

*Larry is **shorter** than most men.*

Comparative Adverb: An adverb involved in a comparative.

*She works **harder** than most regulars.*

Compound Noun: A noun made up of two or more words.

*I need to set up the **meeting room**.*

Compound Tense (or **Compound Verb**): Any verb tense that is made up of two or more words. *See **Perfect Tense**.*

*The blind dog **is running** on the beach.*

Conditional Mood: The mood of a verb used to express an action or event that *would* occur (or *would have* occurred).

*If the babysitter had time, she **would play** the game again.*

Conditional Perfect Tense: A perfect tense used to express a contrary-to-fact action or event that would have occurred if something else did not happen. It is made by a form of the helping verb TO HAVE in the conditional tense plus the past participle.

*The train **would have stopped** if the engineer had seen the warning.*

Conjugated Verb: A specific verb form used to express a verb in a particular tense and mood.

*She **saw** the painting.*

Conjugation: The structure of various verb forms required to express a verb in all of its tenses and moods and for all persons and number combinations. *See appendix B for examples.*

Conjunction: A word that connects clauses, phrases, words, and/or sentences.

*The girl **and** her skateboard were at the park.*

Consonant: Any letter of the alphabet whose pronunciation involves a closing, or constriction, of the vocal channel. Any letter that is not *a, e, i, o, u,* or *y.*

Contraction: A word formed of a shortening and combining of two other words.

*She cannot = She **can't**.*

Declarative Sentence (aka **Statement**): A sentence that declares something and makes an affirmative or negative statement.

My son sings in the shower.

Definite Article: The article (*the*) that indicates a particular, definite noun.

***The** tourists stood at the entrance.*

Demonstrative: A word generally serving as an adjective, an adverb, or a pronoun that points to a particular, definite noun.

*I will have **this** piece.*

Demonstrative Adjective: An adjective that serves as a demonstrative.

*I miss seeing **those** friends.*

Demonstrative Adverb: An adverb that serves as a demonstrative.

*Leave her car **there**.*

Demonstrative Pronoun: A pronoun that replaces a noun previously identified.

*Hand me the <u>papers</u>—**those** on the floor.*

Dependent (aka **Subordinate**) **Clause:** A clause that, by itself, is not a complete sentence and thus does not convey complete meaning and usually begins with a subordinating conjunction or relative pronoun.

While they were watching, the bird flew away.

Descriptive Adjective: An adjective that describes the noun and adds to the meaning of the noun. Color, size, and shape are examples of descriptive attributes.

*A **blue** taxi, A **large** footprint*

Determiners: A special group of adjectives including articles, demonstratives, quantifiers, and possessives that help define the specificity or identity of the noun. Examples include: the definite article *the* (**the** *horse*), the number twelve (**twelve** *drummers*), and a possessive pronoun (**her** *career*).

Diphthong: Two adjacent vowels that are pronounced as one syllable.

*Come here on the d**ou**ble.*

Direct Command: The most common command, where an order is given formally and explicitly.

Eat your lima beans!

Direct Object: A noun or pronoun that receives the action of the verb directly. A direct object generally answers the question *What?* or *When?*

*She ate the **candy**.*

Exclamation (Sentence): A sentence indicating strong feelings or expressed with great emphasis. Exclamation points are used in punctuation.

I have had it!

Feminine Gender: One of two gender categories—the other is masculine. In English, this distinction is primarily relevant with pronouns, which agree in person with their antecedents. *See also **Gender**.*

*Rebecca is working on **her** medical degree.*

First Person: The form of pronoun and verb referring to and agreeing with the person(s) speaking (*I, we*).

I was a space geek when I was young.

Future Perfect Tense: A perfect tense used to express a future action or event completed before another future action or event. It is made by a form of the helping verb TO HAVE in the future tense plus the past participle.

*After this operation, the old man **will have survived** three primary cancers.*

Future Progressive Tense: A compound tense made by a future tense form of the verb TO BE and the present participle (the -*ing* form) to express actions or events in progress at a future time.

*The show **will be ending** before 10:00.*

Future Tense: A simple tense used to express an action or event that will occur in the future.

*The party **will provide** good community introductions.*

Gender: A label for the differentiation of nouns (and the pronouns that refer to them) into masculine and feminine categories. This concept is meaningful in English only with pronouns that refer to nouns. Nowadays, traditional gender pronoun usage is changing to be more inclusive.

*The boy brought **his** soccer ball.*

Gender Agreement: A condition in which the form of a pronoun agrees in gender with the noun to which it refers. *See also **Gender**.*

*Sarah walked the stage to receive **her** diploma. Ben received **his** diploma in the mail.*

Gerund: A present participle (the -*ing* form of the verb) used as a noun.

***Aging** has its pluses and minuses.*

Helping Verb (aka **Auxiliary Verb**): A verb that is used in forming the tenses, moods, and voices of other verbs. A helping verb is used with a conjugated form of another verb to convey the full tense of the verb phrase.

*They **have** plowed that field for the last twenty years.*

Idiom: An expression whose meaning cannot be derived from the literal interpretation of the words. As such, an idiom is not easily translated into another language.

*That job was a **piece of cake**.*

Imperative Mood: The mood of a verb used to denote a command.

Do it now.

Imperative Sentence (aka **Command**): A command is an imperative sentence. It is used to give an order or mandate, affirmatively or negatively, that something be done.

Give me a minute.

Indefinite Article: The articles *a* and *an* that indicate an unspecified person or object.

*I heard **a** bell.*

Indefinite Pronoun: A pronoun that does not refer to a specific person, to a specific time, or to a clearly defined condition such as *any, something, no one.*

Independent (aka **Main**) **Clause:** A clause that conveys complete meaning (and can stand by itself).

The children completed their homework *before dinner.*

Indicative Mood: The mood of a verb used to indicate a statement of fact. It is the most common of the moods.

The legislature passed the bill before leaving town.

Indirect Command: A gentle form of command, usually in the context of telling someone else what a third person should do.

Have your mom call me *when you have a chance.*

Indirect Object: A noun or pronoun that receives the action of the verb indirectly, through an implied preposition *to* or *for*. An indirect object generally answers the question *For Whom?* or *To Whom?*

*The girl gave (**to**) the **dog** a bone.*

Infinitive: The general form of a verb, indicating no subject or number. In English, the infinitive always starts with the word *to*.

to arrive, to see, to conquer

Interjection: An exclamation, usually a word (or short phrase), that ends with an exclamation point.

Outrageous!

Interrogative Adjective: An adjective used to introduce a question.

***What** am I going to say?*

Interrogative Adverb: An adverb used to introduce a question.

***Where** are you hiding?*

Interrogative Mood: The mood of a verb used to indicate a question.

***Did** your guest leave yet?*

Interrogative Pronoun: A pronoun used to introduce a question.

***Who** is laughing now?*

Interrogative Sentence (aka **Question**): A sentence that inquires about something or asks a question.

Where is your friend?

Intransitive Verb: A verb that does not convey action done to something else (and does not require a direct object nor is a linking verb). The action stops with the verb.

*The governor **spoke**.*

Irregular Verb: A verb that does not follow a standard and fully predictable form in its conjugation. *See appendix B for examples.*

***Let's* Command:** A gentle form of command that is presented as a suggestion.

***Let's** go get a pizza.*

Letter: A symbol used in writing with other letters to create a word. English relies on the twenty-six-letter Roman Latin alphabet. *a, b, c . . .*

Lexicon: A word used to refer to the vocabulary of a language (or some field of endeavor).

*The **lexicon** of the English language is extensive.*

Limiting Adjective: An adjective that defines a noun (as opposed to describing a noun), such as one that addresses the size or quantity of a noun.

*There are **several** routes to the destination.*

Linking Verb: A verb that shows a connection between a subject and a subject complement (word, phrase, clause, predicate adjective, or predicate nominative). It does *not* convey action and deals with the senses and states of being. The most common linking verb is the verb TO BE. Others include TO SEEM and TO BECOME.

*Love **is** blind.*

Main Clause: *See **Independent Clause**.*

Masculine Gender: One of two gender categories; the other is feminine. In English, this distinction is primarily relevant with pronouns, which agree in person with their antecedents. *See also **Gender**.*

*Richard proposed, hoping that **his** long-term girlfriend would become **his** wife.*

Modify: An effect of an adjective or adverb in clarifying or explaining the word it refers to or accompanies.

*The place mats were **red**, **white**, and **blue** to match the patriotic theme.*

Mood: The attitude of the speaker to what is being stated, expressed in the form of the verb. There are five different moods in English: indicative, subjunctive, imperative, interrogative, and conditional.

Near Future Condition: A construction using a verb phrase that indicates something that is about to happen.

*The coworkers **are going** out to celebrate.*

Negative Sentence: A sentence that states, with some form of negation, a condition or situation that is not true.

*He **does not** know how to say supercalifragilisticexpialidocious.*

Neuter Demonstrative Pronoun: A pronoun that is used to point to something that is indefinite or unidentified.

***Who** said that?*

Nominalized Adjective: An adjective that is used as a noun. In English, the word *one* or *ones* is usually stated or implied.

*I don't want the red **one**.*

Noun: A word that signifies a person, animal, place, thing, event, idea, or quality.

*The **painting** depicted an **ark** on the high **seas** loaded with **animals**.*

Noun Series: A string of two or more nouns occurring in a sentence.

*Give the baby his **spinner**, **pacifier**, and **blanket**.*

Number: The characteristic indicating quantity—the singularity or plurality—of a noun or pronoun (and in the agreeing forms of associated articles, adjectives, or verbs).

*The four <u>dogs</u> **love** [not loves] their old chew toys best of all.*

Number Adjective (Ordinal): The form of a number indicating the place being occupied in a sequence.

*Judy was the **first** child.*

Number Agreement: A condition requiring that the form of a noun agree in number with a verb and/or that the form of an article, adjective, or pronoun agree in number with the noun it refers to or modifies.

*The <u>tears</u> **stream** down.*

Object: A noun or pronoun (or phrase that serves as either) that is the receiver of the verb's action (direct object), or follows a preposition (object of the preposition), or mentions for whom the action is intended (indirect object).

*He ate his **lunch**.*

Object Case: Case is a grammar term used to describe different contexts for pronouns in a sentence. A pronoun in the object case is called for when the pronoun is a direct object, an indirect object, or an object of a preposition. *See also **Gender**.*

*Jennifer gave **him** (INDIRECT OBJECT) a lesson.*

Object Pronoun: A personal pronoun in the object case that receives the action of the verb or is the object of a preposition.

*The performer gave the guitar to **her**.*

Particle: The general term for a word that does not in itself have meaning but combines with another word to create a phrasal part of speech with new meaning. For example, when the particle *up* is added to the verb *look*, it creates a new verb *look up*.

*Daniela barely had time to **look up** the words before her spelling test began.*

Participle: A form of a verb used in compound tenses. Participles can also function as adjectives or adverbs. There are two types of participles in English verbs: the present participle and the past participle.

		PRESENT PARTICIPLE		PAST PARTICIPLE
TO SEE	→	*seeing*	→	*seen*

		PRESENT PARTICIPLE		PAST PARTICIPLE
TO WALK	→	*walking*	→	*walked*

Parts of Speech: There are eight major parts of speech: nouns, adjectives, pronouns, verbs, adverbs, conjunctions, prepositions, and interjections. (**Note:** *Some authorities separately identify articles and/or determiners as parts of speech. This book treats both of these groups as subsets of adjectives.*)

Passive Voice: A construction in which the subject receives the action of the verb.

*The playlist **was enjoyed** by the critic.*

Past Participle: A past tense form of the verb suggesting completion and is usually used with a helping verb or as an adjective. In English, the past participle usually ends with *-ed* or *-en*.

*The clock has **started**.*

Past Perfect Tense: A perfect tense used to express a past action or event completed before another past action or event. It is made by a form of the helping verb TO HAVE in the simple past plus the past participle.

*His parents **had signaled** their support of his relocation.*

Past Progressive Tense: A compound tense made by a past tense form of the verb TO BE and the present participle to express actions or events in progress at a specific time in the past.

*The winter **was coming**.*

Past Tense (aka **Preterit** and **Simple Past**): A simple verb tense used to express an action or event that occurred in a past time.

*Yesterday, we **went** our separate ways.*

Perfect Tense: A tense formed of two or more words, one of which is a form of the helping verb TO HAVE.

*I **have visited** this town once before.*

Person: The form of the pronoun and verb showing who is referred to. There are three possible persons in English:

> **First:** the person(s) speaking (*I*, *we*)
> **Second:** the person(s) spoken to (*you*)
> **Third:** the person(s) or thing(s) spoken about (*he*, *she*, *it*, *they*)

Personal Pronoun: A pronoun that takes the place of a noun. They are called personal because they stand in for people (aka persons). *See also **Gender**.*

*David is getting a new band together. **He** hopes to be ready to perform in the fall.*

Phrase: A group of two or more related words that, unlike a clause, do not contain both a subject and a verb and cannot be used as a sentence element.

*They went **for a walk**.*

Plural: A condition of a noun (and other words affected by the noun) indicating more than one person or thing.

*There are five **topics** I would like to talk about.*

Possessive Adjective: An adjective that is used to indicate ownership or possession.

*I broke my **friend's** phone.*

Possessive (Adjective) Pronoun: A personal pronoun in the possessive case used to indicate ownership or possession.

*The secret was **hers** to reveal.*

Possessive Case: Case is a grammar term used to describe different contexts for pronouns in a sentence. A pronoun in the possessive case is called for when the pronoun is meant to indicate possession.

*Rustie announced that the Harley offered in the raffle was now **his**.*

Possessive Phrase: A phrase indicating ownership or possession.

*That **wife of mine** is wonderful.*

Predicate: The part of a sentence that has the verb or verb phrase and expresses the action of the sentence or what is said of the subject.

*The football game **ended with no score**.*

Predicate Adjective: An adjective that serves in the predicate after a linking verb and modifies the subject.

*The <u>babysitter</u> is **tired**.*

Predicate Nominative (aka **Subject Complement**): A noun that serves in the predicate after a linking verb and effectively renames the subject.

*That <u>babysitter</u> is my **daughter**.*

Prefix: A word part that is added to the beginning of a word to create a derivative word.

*dis*inherit

Preposition: A word that conveys the relationship of a noun or pronoun to another word in the sentence.

*They met **at** the garden shop.*

Prepositional Phrase: The group of words comprised of a preposition, its object, and any related modifiers.

*She wrote **in her diary**.*

Present Participle (aka **-*ing* Form**): An invariable verb form, having neither gender nor number (unless used as an adjective). It ends in *-ing* and can be used as a verb (with a helping verb), an adjective, or a noun. It expresses an ongoing action.

*My pets are **getting** old.*

Present Perfect Tense: A perfect tense used to express an action or event in the past without reference to a specific time. It is made by a form of the helping verb TO HAVE in the present tense plus the past participle.

*The CEO **has traveled** to fifteen countries this year.*

Present Progressive Tense: A compound tense made by a present tense form of the verb TO BE and the present participle to express actions or events in progress at a specific time in the present.

*The day **is dawning**.*

Present Tense: A simple verb tense used to express an action or event occurring in the present time.

*You now **are** one of us.*

Progressive Tense: A compound tense made by a form of the verb TO BE and the present participle to express actions or events in progress at a specific time in the present, past, or future. *See **Present Progressive Tense** and **Past Progressive Tense**.*

Pronoun: A word used to take the place of a noun or noun-equivalent.

***They** showed **her** to **her** seat.*

Pronoun Case: Case is a grammar term used to describe different contexts for pronouns in a sentence. A pronoun in the **object case** is called for when the pronoun is a direct object, an indirect object, or an object of a preposition. *See also **Gender**.*

*Jennifer gave **him** (INDIRECT OBJECT) a lesson.*

A pronoun in the **subject case** is called for when the pronoun is a subject or predicate nominative.

***She** (SUBJECT) and Jennifer gave a lesson on conjugations in Latin.*

*This is **she** (PREDICATE NOMINATIVE).*

A pronoun in the **possessive case** indicates ownership or possession.

*That book is **mine**.*

Proper Noun: A noun that signifies a very specific thing and is always capitalized in English.

*The **Chicago Bulls** are on the way back.*

Recent Past Condition: A construction using a verb phrase that indicates something that has just happened.

*The clock **has just** struck midnight.*

Reciprocal Pronoun: A pronoun used to indicate the person(s) involved in a mutual action or in a cross-relationship of some sort.

*They supported **each other** in the work.*

Referent: The person, thing, or other noun to which a pronoun refers and takes the place of. *See also **Antecedent**.*

*The skier, **who** broke a leg, is in the hospital.*

Reflexive Pronoun: A pronoun with *-self* used with a reflexive verb to reflect back or refer back to the subject.

*She gave **herself** a manicure.*

Reflexive Verb: A verb that works with a reflexive pronoun to reflect the action of the verb back to the subject.

*She **prepped herself** for the trip.*

Regular Verb: A verb that follows a standard and fully predictable form in its conjugation. *See appendix B for examples.*

Relative Pronoun: A pronoun that introduces dependent noun and adjective clauses.

*She knew the student **who** won the prize.*

Second Person: The form of pronoun and verb referring to and agreeing with the person(s) being spoken to (*you*).

***You** are a natural helper.*

Sentence: A group of words, with at least one independent clause, that expresses a complete thought. There are four types of sentences: declarative, interrogative, imperative, and exclamation. Sentences can also be affirmative or negative.

Simple Tense: Any verb tense made up of a single word.

*The cat **meowed** loudly.*

Singular: A condition of a noun (and other words affected by the noun) indicating oneness, when the word refers to one person or thing.

*That one old **penny** is worth a bundle.*

Soft Command: A gentle form of command, usually in the context of what someone wishes or wants someone else to do.

I wish that you would do the dishes.

Stress: The vocal emphasis given to a syllable or a word to indicate relative prominence in pronunciation. In written communication, stress is not generally indicated, but in reference sources stress is often marked by using capital letters or by using an accent above the stressed word or syllable. The following example, using the verb TO PRESENT, shows the important difference in meaning if the first syllable is stressed when spoken versus the second.

*PRES – ent: She got her dad a **PRES-ent** for Father's Day.*

*pre-SENT: She decided to **pre-SENT** the gift a day early.*

Subject: The noun or pronoun (or phrase that serves as either) that is spoken of in a sentence. In the active voice, the subject is the performer of the action.

*The new **employee** signed all the papers.*

In the passive voice, the subject is the receiver of the action.

*All the **papers** were signed by the new employee.*

Subject Case: Case is a grammar term used to describe different contexts for pronouns in a sentence. A pronoun in the subject case is called for when the pronoun is the subject or predicate nominative of a sentence. *See also **Gender**.*

They (SUBJECT) all arrived at Carol's beach house.

It was I (PREDICATE NOMINATIVE) who called for reservations.

Subject Pronoun: A personal pronoun that serves as the subject of a sentence.

I need to sleep.

Subjunctive Mood: The mood of a verb used to express subjectivity and uncertainty.

*I wish there **were** five meals a day.*

Subordinate Clause: *See **Dependent Clause**.*

Suffix: A word part that is added to the end of a word to create a derivative word.

*suspense**ful***

Superlative: A form of adjectives and adverbs used to establish the highest and lowest of a quality.

*She is the **best** sprinter in the county.*

Superlative Adjective: An adjective involved in a superlative.

*That is the **most beautiful** vista.*

Superlative Adverb: An adverb involved in a superlative.

*He was regarded **most respectfully**.*

Syllable: A unit of spoken language. A word is made up of one or more syllables.

Tense: The form of the verb that indicates the time in which the action of the verb takes place: past, present, or future.

Third Person: The form of pronoun and verb referring to and agreeing with the person(s) or thing(s) being spoken about (*he, she, it, they*).

***She** never went to Paris.*

Transitive Verb: A verb that conveys action done to something else (and requires a direct object).

*Sally **placed** her <u>coffee</u> on the table.*

Verb: A word that expresses an action, an event, a condition, or a state of being.

*Snow **fell** from the sky.*

Verb Phrase: A phrase that works as a verb to convey tense.

*She **has been crying** for an hour.*

Vocabulary: The total collection of words in a language.

Voice: A distinction applied to a sentence to indicate the relationship between the subject and its verb. *See **Active Voice** and **Passive Voice**.*

Vowel: Any letter of the alphabet whose pronunciation is open—that is, does not involve a closing, or constriction, of the vocal channel. The following letters are vowels in English: *a, e, i, o, u,* and *y.*

– APPENDIX B: –
VERB GUIDES

Of the major parts of speech, verbs are the most difficult to master. There are thousands of them and their forms change in relation to person, number, tense, mood, and voice. Many verbs are not "regular"—meaning they do not follow a regular pattern. So there is a great deal to understand and remember. Important information on verbs is provided in chapter 6. To supplement, this appendix gives some key details in quick-access format as an aid to memory and includes:

- Conjugations of the Primary Helping Verbs TO BE, TO HAVE, and TO DO

- 700+ Regular Verbs

- Key Verb Forms of Common Irregular Verbs

CONJUGATIONS OF THE PRIMARY — HELPING VERBS TO BE, TO HAVE, AND TO DO

VERB INFINITIVE	VERB BASE	be	
	PAST TENSE	was, were	
TO BE	PRESENT PARTICIPLE	being	
	PAST PARTICIPLE	been	
	PERSON	**SINGULAR**	**PLURAL**
PRESENT	First	I am	we are
	Second	you are	you are
	Third	he/she/it is	they are
PAST	First	I was	we were
	Second	you were	you were
	Third	he/she/it was	they were
FUTURE	All	I/we/you/he/she/it/they will be	
PRESENT PROGRESSIVE (PRESENT TENSE OF BE + PRESENT PARTICIPLE)	First	I am being	we are being
	Second	you are being	you are being
	Third	he/she/it is being	they are being
PAST PROGRESSIVE (PAST TENSE OF BE + PRESENT PARTICIPLE)	First	I was being	we were being
	Second	you were being	you were being
	Third	he, she, it was being	they were being
FUTURE PROGRESSIVE	All	There is no future progressive form of the verb TO BE	
PRESENT PERFECT (PRESENT TENSE OF HAVE + PAST PARTICIPLE)	First	I have been	we have been
	Second	you have been	you have been
	Third	he, she, it has been	they have been

PAST PERFECT (PAST TENSE OF HAVE + PAST PARTICIPLE)	All	I, we, you, he, she, it, they **had been**
FUTURE PERFECT (FUTURE TENSE OF HAVE + PAST PARTICIPLE)	All	I, we, you, he, she, it, they **will have been**
PRESENT PERFECT PROGRESSIVE		
PAST PERFECT PROGRESSIVE	There are no perfect progressive forms of the verb **TO BE**	
FUTURE PERFECT PROGRESSIVE		

VERB INFINITIVE TO HAVE	VERB BASE	have	
	PAST TENSE	had	
	PRESENT PARTICIPLE	having	
	PAST PARTICIPLE	had	
	PERSON	**SINGULAR**	**PLURAL**
PRESENT	First	I have	we have
	Second	you have	you have
	Third	he/she/it has	they have
PAST	All	I/we/you/he/she/it/they had	
FUTURE	All	I/we/you/he/she/it/they will have	
PRESENT PROGRESSIVE (PRESENT TENSE OF BE + PRESENT PARTICIPLE)	First	I am having	we are having
	Second	you are having	you are having
	Third	he/she/it is having	they are having
PAST PROGRESSIVE (PAST TENSE OF BE + PRESENT PARTICIPLE)	First	I was having	we were having
	Second	you were having	you were having
	Third	he, she, it was having	they were having
FUTURE PROGRESSIVE (FUTURE TENSE OF BE + PRESENT PARTICIPLE)	All	I/we/you/he/she/it/they will be having	
PRESENT PERFECT (PRESENT TENSE OF HAVE + PAST PARTICIPLE)	First	I have had	we have had
	Second	you have had	you have had
	Third	he, she, it has had	they have had
PAST PERFECT (PAST TENSE OF HAVE + PAST PARTICIPLE)	All	I, we, you, he, she, it, they had had	
FUTURE PERFECT (FUTURE TENSE OF HAVE + PAST PARTICIPLE)	All	I, we, you, he, she, it, they will have had	

		First	I have been having	we have been having
PRESENT PERFECT PROGRESSIVE (PRESENT PERFECT TENSE OF BE + PRESENT PARTICIPLE)		Second	you have been having	you have been having
		Third	he, she, it has been having	they have been having
PAST PERFECT PROGRESSIVE (PAST PERFECT TENSE OF BE + PRESENT PARTICIPLE)		All	I, we, you, he, she, it, they had been having	
FUTURE PERFECT PROGRESSIVE (FUTURE PERFECT TENSE OF BE + PRESENT PARTICIPLE)		All	I, we, you, he, she, it, they will have been having	

	VERB BASE	do	
VERB INFINITIVE TO DO	**PAST TENSE**	did	
	PRESENT PARTICIPLE	doing	
	PAST PARTICIPLE	done	
	PERSON	**SINGULAR**	**PLURAL**
PRESENT	First	I do	we do
	Second	you do	you do
	Third	he/she/it does	they do
PAST	All	I/we/you/he/she/it/they did	
FUTURE	All	I/we/you/he/she/it/they will do	
PRESENT PROGRESSIVE (PRESENT TENSE OF BE + PRESENT PARTICIPLE)	First	I am doing	we are doing
	Second	you are doing	you are doing
	Third	he/she/it is doing	they are doing
PAST PROGRESSIVE (PAST TENSE OF BE + PRESENT PARTICIPLE)	First	I was doing	we were doing
	Second	you were doing	you were doing
	Third	he, she, it was doing	they were doing

FUTURE PROGRESSIVE (FUTURE TENSE OF BE + PRESENT PARTICIPLE)	All	I/we/you/he/she/it/they will be doing	
PRESENT PERFECT (PRESENT TENSE OF HAVE + PAST PARTICIPLE)	First	I have done	we have done
	Second	you have done	you have done
	Third	he, she, it has done	they have done
PAST PERFECT (PAST TENSE OF HAVE + PAST PARTICIPLE)	All	I, we, you, he, she, it, they had done	
FUTURE PERFECT (FUTURE TENSE OF HAVE + PAST PARTICIPLE)	All	I, we, you, he, she, it, they will have done	
PRESENT PERFECT PROGRESSIVE (PRESENT PERFECT TENSE OF BE + PRESENT PARTICIPLE)	First	I have been doing	we have been doing
	Second	you have been doing	you have been doing
	Third	he, she, it has been doing	they have been doing
PAST PERFECT PROGRESSIVE (PAST PERFECT TENSE OF BE + PRESENT PARTICIPLE)	All	I, we, you, he, she, it, they had been doing	
FUTURE PERFECT PROGRESSIVE (FUTURE PERFECT TENSE OF BE + PRESENT PARTICIPLE)	All	I, we, you, he, she, it, they will have been doing	

– 700+ REGULAR VERBS –
(IN ALPHABETICAL ORDER)

Regular verbs are called *regular* because their conjugations follow a "regular" (common) pattern. With any verb base form selected from the alphabetical listing on the following pages, you can follow the rules for regular verbs to create the conjugation for the verb. These rules, along with a conjugation template and rules for handling spelling variations, are provided in chapter 6. Use this list to identify common verbs that are regular in construction.

A abandon, accept, accompany, accustom, achieve, act, add, address, admire, admit, adopt, advertise, advise, afford, agree, aid, alert, allow, amuse, analyze, announce, annoy, answer, apologize, appeal, appear, applaud, appreciate, approach, approve, argue, arrange, arrest, arrive, ask, assist, attach, attack, attempt, attend, attract, avoid

B back, bake, balance, ban, bang, banish, bare, bark, base, bat, bathe, battle, beam, beg, behave, believe, belong, bleach, bless, blind, blink, blot, blush, board, boast, boil, bolt, bomb, book, boost, bore, borrow, bounce, bow, box, brake, branch, breathe, bruise, brush, bubble, bump, burn, bury, buzz

C calculate, call, camp, care, carry, carve, cause, challenge, change, charge, chase, cheat, check, cheer, chew, choke, chop, claim, clap, clean, clear, climb, clip, close, coach, coil, collect, color, comb, command, communicate, compare, compete, complain, complete, concentrate, concern, confess, confuse, connect, consider, consist, construct, contain, continue, control, cook, cool, copy, correct, cough, count, cover, crack, crash, craw, crawl, create, cross, crush, cry, cure, curl, curve, cycle

D dam, damage, dance, dare, decay, deceive, decide, declare, decorate, delay, delight, deliver, deny, depend, describe, desert, deserve, destroy, detect, determine, develop, dial, die, dine, disagree, disappear, disapprove, disarm, discover, dislike, disturb, divide, double, doubt, drag, drain, dress, drip, drop, drown, drum, dry, dust

E earn, ease, educate, eliminate, embarrass, employ, empty, enclose, encourage, end, engage, enjoy, enter, entertain, envy, erase, escape, establish, estimate, examine, exchange, excite, exclaim, excuse, exercise, exist, expand, expect, explain, explode, express, extend

F face, fade, fail, fancy, fasten, fax, fear, fence, fetch, file, fill, film, finish, fire, fish, fit, fix, flap, flash, float, flood, flow, flower, focus, fold, follow, fool, force, form, found, frame, freeze, frighten, frighten, fry

G gain, gather, gaze, glow, glue, grab, grate, grease, greet, grin, grip, groan, guarantee, guard, guess, guide

H hammer, hand, handle, hang, happen, harass, harm, hate, haunt, head, heal, heap, heat, help, hook, hop, hope, hover, hug, hum, hunt, hurry

I identify, ignore, imagine, impress, improve, include, increase, indicate, influence, inform, inject, injure, instruct, intend, interest, interfere, interrupt, introduce, invent, invite, involve, iron, irritate, itch

J jail, jam, jog, join, joke, judge, juggle, jump

K kick, kill, kiss, kneel, knit, knock, knot

L label, land, last, laugh, launch, lay, leak, learn, level, license, lick, lie, lighten, like, list, listen, live, load, lock, long, look, love

M man, manage, march, mark, marry, massage, match, mate, matter, measure, meddle, melt, memorize, mend, mess up, milk, mine, miss, mix, moan, moor, mourn, move, muddle, mug, multiply, murder

N nail, name, need, nest, nod, note, notice, number

O obey, object, observe, obtain, occur, offend, offer, open, order, organize, overflow, owe, own

P pack, paddle, paint, park, part, pass, paste, pat, pause, peck, pedal, peel, peep, perform, permit, persuade, phone, pick, pinch, pine, place, plan, plant, play, please, plough, plug, point, poke, polish, pop, possess, post, pour, practice, pray, preach, precede, prefer, prepare, present, preserve, press, pretend, prevent, prick, print, produce, program, promise, pronounce, protect, provide, pull, pump, punch, puncture, punish, purchase, push

Q question, quiver, quote

R race, radiate, rain, raise, reach, realize, receive, recognize, record, reduce, reflect, refuse, register, regret, reign, reject, rejoice, relax, release, rely, remain, remember, remind, remove, repair, repeat, replace, reply, report, represent, reproduce, request, require, rescue, reserve, resolve, rest, retire, return, review, rhyme, rinse, risk, rob, rock, roll, rot, row, rub, ruin, rule, rush

S sack, sail, satisfy, save, saw, scare, scatter, scold, scorch, scrape, scratch, scream, screw, scribble, scrub, seal, search, seem, select, separate, serve, settle, shade, share, shave, shelter, shiver, shock, shop, shrug, sigh, sign, signal, sin, sip, ski, skip, slap, slip, slow, smash, smell, smile, smoke, snatch, sneeze, sniff, snore, snow, soak, soothe, sound, spare, spark, sparkle, spell, spill, spoil, spot, spray, sprout, squash, squeak, squeal, squeeze, stage, stain, stamp, stare, start, stay, steer, step, stir, stitch, stop, store, strap, strengthen, stretch, strip, stroke, study, stuff, subtract, succeed, suck, suffer, suggest, suit, supply, support, suppose, surprise, surround, suspect, suspend, swallow, switch

T tackle, talk, tame, tap, taste, tease, telephone, tempt, terrify, test, thank, thaw, tick, tickle, tie, time, tip, tire, touch, tour, tow, trace, trade, train, transport, trap, travel, treat, tremble, trick, trip, trot, trouble, trust, try, tug, tumble, turn, twist, type

U underline, undress, unfasten, unite, unlock, unpack, untidy, use

V vanish, visit

W wail, wait, walk, wander, want, warm, warn, wash, waste, watch, water, wave, weigh, welcome, whine, whip, whirl, whisper, whistle, wink, wipe, wish, wobble, wonder, work, worry, wrap, wreck, wrestle, wriggle

X x-ray

Y yawn, yell

Z zip, zoom

– KEY VERB FORMS –
OF COMMON IRREGULAR VERBS

Unlike regular verbs, *irregular* verbs do not follow a common conjugation pattern. They deviate in one or more respects from regular verbs, and the deviations are often in the key verb forms. In the following pages, the key verb forms are shown for:

- Primary Helping Verbs

- Frequently Used Irregular Verbs

- Other Common Irregular Verbs

Note that the five key verb forms are identified, from which full conjugations can be developed: 1. Infinitive, 2. Base, 3. Simple Past, 4. Present Participle, and 5. Past Participle.

PRIMARY HELPING VERBS

INFINITIVE	BASE	SIMPLE PAST	PRESENT PARTICIPLE	PAST PARTICIPLE
TO BE	be	was, were	being	been
TO DO	do	did	doing	done
TO HAVE	have	had	having	had

FREQUENTLY USED IRREGULAR VERBS

INFINITIVE	BASE	SIMPLE PAST	PRESENT PARTICIPLE	PAST PARTICIPLE
TO BEGIN	begin	began	beginning	begun
TO BRING	bring	brought	bringing	brought
TO COME	come	came	coming	come
TO EAT	eat	ate	eating	eaten
TO FEEL	feel	felt	feeling	felt
TO FIND	find	found	finding	found
TO GET	get	got	getting	gotten
TO GIVE	give	gave	giving	given
TO GO	go	went	going	gone
TO KNOW	know	knew	knowing	known
TO LEAVE	leave	left	leaving	left
TO MAKE	make	made	making	made
TO PUT	put	put	putting	put
TO SAY	say	said	saying	said
TO SEE	see	saw	seeing	seen
TO SHOW	show	showed	showing	shown/showed
TO TAKE	take	took	taking	taken
TO TELL	tell	told	telling	told
TO THINK	think	thought	thinking	thought
TO WRITE	write	wrote	writing	written

OTHER COMMON IRREGULAR VERBS

INFINITIVE	BASE	SIMPLE PAST	PRESENT PARTICIPLE	PAST PARTICIPLE
TO ARISE	arise	arose	arising	arisen
TO AWAKE	awake	awoke, awaked	awaking	awoken, awaked
TO BEAR	bear	bore	bearing	born
TO BEAT	beat	beat	beating	beaten, beat
TO BECOME	become	became	becoming	become
TO BEND	bend	bent	bending	bent
TO BEREAVE	bereave	bereaved, bereft	bereaving	bereaved, bereft
TO BET	bet	bet, betted	betting	bet, betted
TO BID	bid	bade, bid	bidding	bidden, bid, bade
TO BIND	bind	bound	binding	bound
TO BITE	bite	bit	biting	bitten
TO BLEED	bleed	bled	bleeding	bled
TO BLESS	bless	blessed, blest	blessing	blessed, blest
TO BLOW	blow	blew	blowing	blown
TO BREAK	break	broke	breaking	broken
TO BREED	breed	bred	breeding	bred
TO BUILD	build	built	building	built
TO BURN	burn	burned, burnt	burning	burned, burnt
TO BURST	burst	burst	bursting	burst
TO BUY	buy	bought	buying	bought
TO CATCH	catch	caught	catching	caught
TO CHOOSE	choose	chose	choosing	chosen
TO CLING	cling	clung	clinging	clung
TO CLOTHE	clothe	clothed, clad	clothing	clothed, clad
TO COST	cost	cost	costing	cost
TO CREEP	creep	crept	creeping	crept

TO CUT	cut	cut	cutting	cut
TO DEAL	deal	dealt	dealing	dealt
TO DIG	dig	dug	digging	dug
TO DRAW	draw	drew	drawing	drawn
TO DREAM	dream	dreamed, dreamt	dreaming	dreamed, dreamt
TO DRINK	drink	drank	drinking	drunk
TO DRIVE	drive	drove	driving	driven
TO DWELL	dwell	dwelled, dwelt	dwelling	dwelled, dwelt
TO FALL	fall	fell	falling	fallen
TO FEED	feed	fed	feeding	fed
TO FIGHT	fight	fought	fighting	fought
TO FLEE	flee	fled	fleeing	fled
TO FLING	fling	flung	flinging	flung
TO FLY	fly	flew	flying	flown
TO FORBID	forbid	forbad, forbade	forbidding	forbid, forbidden
TO FORECAST	forecast	forecast, forecasted	forecasting	forecast, forecasted
TO FORGET	forget	forgot	forgetting	forgotten
TO FREEZE	freeze	froze	freezing	frozen
TO GRIND	grind	ground	grinding	ground
TO GRIP	grip	gripped	gripping	gripped
TO GROW	grow	grew	growing	grown
TO HANG	hang	hung	hanging	hung
TO HEAR	hear	heard	hearing	heard
TO HEAVE	heave	heaved, hove	heaving	heaved, hove
TO HIDE	hide	hid	hiding	hidden, hid
TO HIT	hit	hit	hitting	hit
TO HOLD	hold	held	holding	held
TO HURT	hurt	hurt	hurting	hurt
TO KEEP	keep	kept	keeping	kept
TO KNEEL	kneel	kneeled, knelt	kneeling	kneeled, knelt
TO KNIT	knit	knitted, knit	knitting	knitted, knit

TO LAY	lay	laid	laying	laid
TO LEAD	lead	led	leading	led
TO LEAP	leap	leaped, leapt	leaping	leaped, leapt
TO LEARN	learn	learned	learning	learned
TO LEND	lend	lent	lending	lent
TO LET	let	let	letting	let
TO LIE	lie	lay	lying	lain
TO LIGHT	light	lit, lighted	lighting	lit, lighted
TO LOSE	lose	lost	losing	lost
TO MEAN	mean	meant	meaning	meant
TO MEET	meet	met	meeting	met
TO MELT	melt	melted	melting	molten, melted
TO MOW	mow	mowed	mowing	mown, mowed
TO PAY	pay	paid	paying	paid
TO PLEAD	plead	pled, pleaded	pleading	pled, pleaded
TO PROVE	prove	proved	proving	proven, proved
TO QUIT	quit	quit, quitted	quitting	quit, quitted
TO READ	read	read	reading	read
TO RID	rid	rid, ridded	ridding	rid, ridded
TO RIDE	ride	rode	riding	ridden
TO RING	ring	rang	ringing	rung
TO RISE	rise	rose	rising	risen
TO RUN	run	ran	running	run
TO SEEK	seek	sought	seeking	sought
TO SELL	sell	sold	selling	sold
TO SEND	send	sent	sending	sent
TO SET	set	set	setting	set
TO SEW	sew	sewed	sewing	sewn, sewed
TO SHAKE	shake	shook	shaking	shaken
TO SHEAR	shear	sheared	shearing	shorn, sheared
TO SHED	shed	shed	shedding	shed
TO SHINE	shine	shone/shined	shining	shone/shined
TO SHOE	shoe	shod, shoed	shoeing	shod, shoed

TO SHOOT	shoot	shot	shooting	shot
TO SHRED	shred	shred, shredded	shredding	shred, shredded
TO SHRINK	shrink	shrank, shrunk	shrinking	shrunk
TO SHUT	shut	shut	shutting	shut
TO SING	sing	sang	singing	sung
TO SINK	sink	sank	sinking	sunk
TO SIT	sit	sat	sitting	sat
TO SLEEP	sleep	slept	sleeping	slept
TO SLIDE	slide	slid	sliding	slid
TO SLING	sling	slung	slinging	slung
TO SLINK	slink	slunk	slinking	slunk
TO SLIT	slit	slit	slitting	slit
TO SOW	sow	sowed	sowing	sown, sowed
TO SPEAK	speak	spoke	speaking	spoken
TO SPEED	speed	sped, speeded	speeding	sped, speeded
TO SPEND	spend	spent	spending	spent
TO SPIN	spin	spun	spinning	spun
TO SPIT	spit	spat	spitting	spat
TO SPLIT	split	split	splitting	split
TO SPREAD	spread	spread	spreading	spread
TO SPRING	spring	sprang, sprung	springing	sprung
TO STAND	stand	stood	standing	stood
TO STEAL	steal	stole	stealing	stolen
TO STICK	stick	stuck	sticking	stuck
TO STING	sting	stung	stinging	stung
TO STINK	stink	stank, stunk	stinking	stunk
TO STRIDE	stride	strode	striding	stridden
TO STRIKE	strike	struck	striking	struck
TO SWEAR	swear	swore	swearing	sworn
TO SWEAT	sweat	sweat, sweated	sweating	sweat, sweated
TO SWEEP	sweep	swept	sweeping	swept
TO SWELL	swell	swelled	swelling	swollen, swelled

TO SWIM	swim	swam	swimming	swum
TO SWING	swing	swung	swinging	swung
TO TEACH	teach	taught	teaching	taught
TO TEAR	tear	tore	tearing	torn
TO THINK	think	thought	thinking	thought
TO THROW	throw	threw	throwing	thrown
TO THRUST	thrust	thrust	thrusting	thrust
TO TREAD	tread	trod	treading	trodden
TO WAKE	wake	woke, waked	waking	woken, waked
TO WEAR	wear	wore	wearing	worn
TO WEAVE	weave	wove	weaving	woven
TO WED	wed	wed, wedded	wedding	wed, wedded
TO WEEP	weep	wept	weeping	wept
TO WET	wet	wet, wetted	wetting	wet, wetted
TO WIN	win	won	winning	won
TO WIND	wind	wound	winding	wound
TO WRING	wring	wrung	wringing	wrung

– APPENDIX C: –
USEFUL GRAMMAR RESOURCES

There are many sources available on the many different aspects of grammar. The following publications are especially insightful.

The Associated Press. *The Associated Press Stylebook*, 2019. Associated Press, 2019.

Barrett, Grant. *Perfect English Grammar: Indispensable Guide*. Zephyros Press, 2016.

Casagrande, June. *Joy of Syntax*. Ten Speed Press, 2018.

Collins, Tim. *Correct Your English Errors*, 2nd Edition. McGraw-Hill, 2018.

Dreyer, Benjamin. *Dreyer's English: An Utterly Correct Guide to Clarity & Style*. Random House, 2019.

Farlex International. *Complete English Grammar Rules*. Farlex International, 2017.

Seely, John. *Everyday Grammar*. Oxford University Press, 2004.

Shertzer, Margaret D. *Elements of Grammar*. Macmillan, 1986.

Strauss, Jane, and Lester Kaufman, et al. *The Blue Book of Grammar and Punctuation*, 11th Edition. Wiley, 2014.

Strunk Jr., William, and Richard De A'Morelli. *Elements of Style: Classic Edition*. Spectrum Ink Publishing, 2018.

Swan, Michael. *Swan's Practical English Usage*, 4th Edition. Oxford University Press, 2017.

Thurman, Susan. *The Only Grammar Book You'll Ever Need*. Adams Media, 2003.

Troyka, Lynn Quitman, and Doug Hesse. *Simon & Schuster Handbook for Writers*, 11th Edition. Simon & Schuster, 2016.

The University of Chicago Press Editorial Staff. *The Chicago Manual of Style*, 17th Edition. The University of Chicago, 2017.

Vitto, Cindy L. *Grammar by Diagram*. Broadview Press Ltd., 2003.

Watson, Cecelia. *Semicolon: Past, Present & Future*. HarperCollins, 2019.

Woods, Geraldine. *English Grammar for Dummies*, 3rd Edition. John Wiley & Sons, 2017.

− ACKNOWLEDGMENTS −

Many thanks to my colleagues at Quarto Publishing—Publisher Rage Kindelsperger, Creative Director Laura Drew, Managing Editor Cara Donaldson, Designer Amelia LeBarron, and Senior Editor John Foster. *Everyday Grammar Made Easy* is their brainchild, and I was fortunate to be selected to carry the project forward. Rage provided steady leadership along the way and John, as editor, served as mentor, coach, as well as collaborator. I am especially grateful for his counsel and project management that steered the work to a successful conclusion.

− ABOUT THE AUTHOR −

Rod Mebane is known for his ability to simplify complex things and to present them in compelling ways. In the early 1990s, while living in Dallas, Rod decided to study Spanish at a local community college and (for *fun*) published *Más Fácil*, a Prentice Hall textbook containing the rules of Spanish grammar in less than one hundred pages of text. In 2021, Rod's professional grammar focus broadened to include English with this publication of *Everyday Grammar Made Easy*.

Exceptional analytical and presentation skills have served Rod well in his career—one that is anchored by a number of significant positions, including University Treasurer (Southern Methodist University), Foundation Director (MacArthur Foundation), Chief Learning Officer (BDO USA), and Consulting Partner. He also earned degrees from Swarthmore College and University of Pennsylvania's Annenberg School for Communication. Along this trek, Rod honed his communication knowledge and skills and now offers a variety of communication support services under the banner of Wordsmith Associates.

In the wordsmith capacity, Rod has published a variety of works, spanning the fields of education, investment and finance, and professional development. He has also helped numerous individuals realize their authoring dreams, enabling them to publish their stories—usually in the form of reflective, later-in-life documents (including letters, memoirs, and tributes).

Rod lives with his wife, Donna, and blind dog, Willie, in Geneva, Illinois, a western suburb of Chicago. When pursuing avocational interests, Rod can be found carving wood, championing honeybees, and nurturing his family tree.

- INDEX -